There was a need for non-attachment, to be sure; but also a prerequisite of knife-like resolve. It was as if, here in this distant, exotic land, we were compelled to raise the art of shopping to an experience that was, on the one hand, detached and almost Zen—our ultimate goal was, after all, enlightenment—and, on the other hand, tinged with desperation, like shopping at Macy's or Bloomingdale's during a one-day-only White Sale. . . .

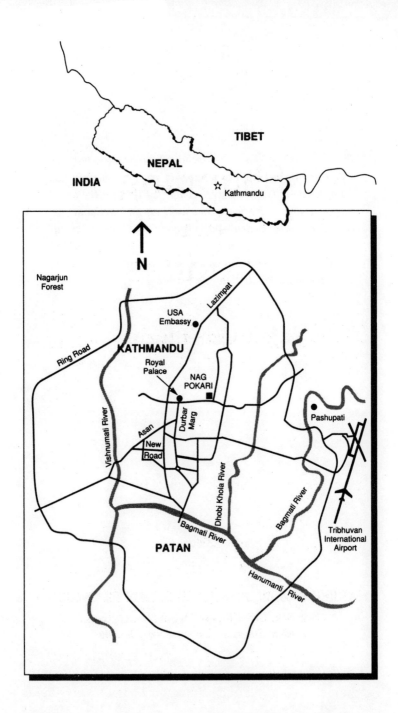

Shopping
for
Buddhas

Jeff Greenwald

1817

HARPER & ROW, PUBLISHERS, SAN FRANCISCO

New York, Grand Rapids, Philadelphia, St. Louis
London, Singapore, Sydney, Tokyo, Toronto

To my mother

SHOPPING FOR BUDDHAS. Copyright © 1990 by Jeff Greenwald. All
rights reserved. Printed in the United States of America.
No part of this book may be used or reproduced in any manner
whatsoever without written permission except in the case of
brief quotations embodied in critical articles and reviews.
For information, address Harper & Row, Publishers, Inc.,
10 East 53rd Street, New York, NY 10022.

FIRST EDITION

Library of Congress Cataloging-in-Publication Data

Greenwald, Jeff
    Shopping for Buddhas / Jeff Greenwald—1st ed.
        p.   cm.
    ISBN 0-06-250358-8
        1. Himalaya Mountains Region—Description and travel.
2. Himalaya Mountains Region—Religion.   3. Greenwald, Jeff,
1954-   Journeys—Himalaya Mountains Region.   I. Title.
DS485.H6G72   1990
915.49604—dc20   89-46152
                                                               CIP

90 91 92 93 94 FAIR 10 9 8 7 6 5 4 3 2 1

This edition is printed on acid-free paper that meets the
American National Standards Institute Z39.48 Standard.

Acknowledgments

I owe a debt of gratitude to the many exceptional friends, supporters, and spiritual allies who helped bring *Shopping for Buddhas* to life—first as a performed monologue, and ultimately as this book.

First, of course, I wish to greet the people who actually participated in these various and sundry excursions, adventures, and shopping sprees. Rick Gaynor and Nancy Lindborg were my great friends and traveling companions in Nepal and Tibet; Ray Rodney offered me the hospitality of his lovely Snake Lake compound, where I conceived and completed this book; and Karen Nuñez, intrepid traveler, joined me as sweet Shakti and smart shopper extraordinaire.

I extend a cup of hot *rakshi* to toast Elliot Marseille, who for five years helped direct the SEVA Foundation's marvelous eye care program in southern Nepal; to Ani Marilyn, for the gift of her humor, wisdom, and generosity; and to Lalji, whose keen insight and droll wit have kept me gleefully off balance for a good ten years.

Thanks also to Jim Goodman, Mukunda Aryal, and to Padam Thakurathi, a journalist whose personal courage and commitment to his country have added profoundly to this book. Grateful acknowledgment is given to Bukkyo Dendo Kyokai for permission to reprint sections of *The Teaching of Buddha*. I must also express my gratitude to the *Rising Nepal*, which allowed me to reprint a few letters and articles from their pages; and to the United States Embassy in Kathmandu, for helping me get a handle on the human rights situation in Nepal.

Numerous other friends and artists inspired me in various phases of the writing. I especially want to thank World Media Warrior Rob Brezsny, John O'Keeffe, Richard Kohn, Scoop Nisker, Jen Schwerin, V. Carroll Dunham, Thomas Kelly, Diane Summers, Diane Siegal, Ken Doud, Sheila Davies, John Miller, Louis B. Jones, and Roxy Lippel.

Shopping for Buddhas was originally conceived, in much shorter form, for the stage. It was the first time I had ever attempted this sort of thing, and my immediate discovery was that theater work is about fifty times more complicated than one would imagine. I could not have pulled it off alone.

Aram Amadeus Gerstein—advisor, director, stage manager, sound man, and Well of Patience—was the one who convinced me to write it all down in the first place. "What I owe you" (as Alec Guinness tells Peter O'Toole at the end of *Lawrence of Arabia*) "is beyond evaluation." Thanks also to Shelly Ruston at the Santa Barbara Museum of Art, Roberto Bedoya at San Francisco's Intersection for the Arts, artist/composer Jun Ishimuro, and Tim Hansen and Arnie Passman of the Julia Morgan Theater in Berkeley. If opening night at Intersection sold out, it was thanks in large part to the faith and friendship of Don George, maverick travel editor of the *San Francisco Examiner*. Tod Elkins got that crazy evening on video; I appreciate it.

Finally, I wish to thank the four people most directly responsible for shaping *Shopping for Buddhas* into its present incarnation. Shoshana Tembeck Alexander, whiz-kid networker, put the process in motion by recommending the original monologue to her friends at Harper & Row. Alexandra Pitcher, poetess and mystical twin, edited the very first draft; Hilary Vartanian of Harper & Row offered innumerable excellent comments on the revised manuscript; and Mark Salzwedel, my editor, continues to improve the book with his ability to see beyond the obvious and into the realms of the subtle.

To these people, and the many other allies who remain unmentioned, I offer my gratitude. But my ultimate expression of appreciation goes to the people of Nepal—whose warmth, hospitality, and profound spirituality have had such a vast and unexpected influence on this particular lifetime. Please accept my humble, heartfelt, and inexpressibly grateful *Namasté*.

I was one of them, shopping, at last.

DON DELILLO, *White Noise*

"Hello. You've reached the mass of cells, nerves, hormones, and protoplasm that compose the human being known as Jeff Greenwald. This entity is currently at large on Earth, struggling against the demons of greed, envy, and desire. If you wish to leave a message, . . . here is the beep."

"Hi, honey, this is Mom. I just wanted to tell you that I ran into Tanya Edelstein at Walbaum's the other day, and she told me that her son Morty just got this incredible job, photographing locations in Nepal and India for a new movie. They're paying him something like $5,000 a week. Ach! I only wish it could be you!

"Anyway, everything's the same here. Nothing new. Love you. . . ."

1

Lord Buddha said,
"This is true suffering; this is true cause; this is true cessation; this is the true path.
"Know the sufferings; give up their causes; attain the cessation of suffering; follow the true path.
"Know the sufferings although there is nothing to know; relinquish the causes of misery although there is nothing to relinquish; be earnest in cessation although there is nothing to cease; practice the means of following the true path although there is nothing to practice."
—BUKKYO DENDO KYOKAI, *The Teaching of Buddha*

On the morning of Monday, October 19, 1987, I woke up at a place called Gosainkund—a pocket of sacred lakes, dedicated to Lord Shiva, some 14,300 feet high in the Nepali Himalayas.

I'd made the trek up to this holy site with Karen, my stateside lover, who had flown from California to visit me in Nepal for a few weeks. We spent the first spectacular evening performing a *kora*—a devotional, clockwise circuit around the lake—pausing every few minutes to stare west, over the panorama of cloud-shrouded mountains that emerged into the sky. "It looks like Heaven," Karen said. I could see what she meant; how the bolts of sunlight pierced through the clouds and spread like an oriental fan across the spine of the Himalayas, illuminating the vapors trapped below.

Our accommodations in the one-room Gosainkund Lodge were basic: straw mats on a stone floor. We inflated our air mattresses, ate some Chinese noodles, and climbed into our bags to sleep.

Sometime during the night, the wind picked up. It began as a low drone, rising and falling with an ominous cadence—like the voices of monks in a tantric choir. We felt icy particles alight and melt on our cheeks and noses, exposed from the maws of our mummy bags. Once during the night I woke up, bladder twitching, and felt around. It was weird—everything seemed wet and cold. I flopped back down, damned if I was going to go outside to piss.

I remember the fatal moment when I opened my eyes and saw that the lodge was full of snow. It had blown right in under the roof and covered us, our gear, our bags, everything. Karen went outside and shrieked—the place was buried, waist deep in snow, and it was still falling, blowing in furiously, gusting through the shutters and under the roof, an icy, biting, relentless blizzard.

What to do? Wait at Gosainkund, this tiny way station at 14,000 feet and risk being marooned forever? Or attempt the descent, along cliff-hanging mountain trails, in a blinding snowstorm?

Our porter tried leaving, dressed in tennies and Karen's socks, with a woolen blanket wrapped around his shoulders, and returned after five minutes. *Saakdaina*—"Impossible." The path was utterly invisible, totally snowbound. An hour or two later another Nepali came staggering in. He brought horrible news. There was a dead woman on the trail, he said. Frozen. She'd been on her way to Gosainkund last night, when the storm hit. . . .

But Gosainkund was no place to hang around. Here it was, 6:30 A.M., and we already felt as if we'd been stuck in

4

that cramped, frigid little stone hut forever. The storm might let up in ten minutes; it might rage for a week. In the latter case, we could just as easily die of sheer boredom. . . .

Clearly, there was no alternative. So, joining forces with a similarly marooned Swiss couple—two beefy, strapping Aryans—their porter, and ours, we bundled ourselves up in every last bit of clothing we had brought and set off down the mountain.

The first hundred steps were sheer panic. Snow up to our crotches; stumbling, falling, trying to follow the deep blue footprints left by the Swiss couple plowing on up ahead. The path had been so magnificent yesterday morning—now it was Death's cakewalk. Karen was nearly hysterical at first, blindly blundering along, an L.A. girl consummately out of her element. As were we all.

But the worst was yet to come. Rounding the edge of the lake, we found ourselves on a high, unprotected ridge. The wind howled furiously, blinding us with ice needles, trying with all its might to blow us off the mountain, over the sheer drop that lay some six feet to our left. Left hand frozen, eyes frozen, frozen snot cracking off my face, I clung desperately to the back of Karen's pack as the wind shoved her pitilessly toward the edge of the universe.

In the distance, beyond a white haze, I could see the hardy Swiss couple vanishing from sight. They plowed determinedly onward—followed by our pathetically attired porter, whose meager blanket whipped uselessly across his thin shoulders.

Above our heads, dead birds, wings broken and shredded, flew through the air like shrapnel. I gripped Karen's hand with numb fingers as we cut down from the ridge and turned directly into the blinding snow, tripping and falling every other step. At one point I just lay there, spread-eagled, like a drowning man—ready to give it all up. To just surrender, stop fighting this terrible deluge.

5

But no—we hauled ourselves up, convinced that we could reach the first teahouse, another half-hour at most—we could see it, a safe haven of boiled water and shelter, far, far below.

We stumbled onward, praying and rolling down the mountainside, and arrived just in time to see the roof blowing off, and the little family that lived there fleeing for their lives, with all their belongings, including three children, strapped to their backs.

There was no more path, no more objective reality at all. I watched, stunned, as the Sherpa family leaped into the river—a raging, muddy torrent—and ran with it. They knew, in their infinite mountain wisdom, that it was flowing down, down—and down was where we wanted to go. We followed them, running blindly, slipping over frozen stones in animal panic.

An eternity later, we arrived in the village of Sing Ghompa. We had dropped thousands of feet; it was pouring rain. There were two rooms left at the lodge. We fell in out of the storm, into the dining hall, and immediately met the dazed, disbelieving stares of thirty Israeli trekkers, who were drinking rakshi and singing Hebrew folk songs. The Swiss couple vanished immediately. Karen and I drank tea and ate chocolate, finally building up the strength to crawl down the hill to our room.

Not a single thing in our packs had remained dry: socks, cameras, Band-Aids, batteries—everything was drenched through and through. We hung our soaking wet clothes over every surface and collapsed, utterly spent, onto our cots.

Lucky, so very lucky to be alive.

"Goddamit!" I hollered.
"What's wrong?!?" Karen looked at me in a panic.

"Look at the foam pads they put on these cots! Jesus—they're thin as shit! We had such nice, thick ones in that upstairs room, two days ago. What a ripoff! How do they expect us to sleep on these?!"

As soon as we got back to Kathmandu, we heard about the stock-market crash. It had occurred on Black Monday, the very same day that we had almost lost our lives in the storm—one of the worst storms to hit Nepal in recorded history.

At that moment I was enlightened, and realized: "life and wealth are transitory. The only way to protect yourself against these implacable truths is to invest in Buddhas. That way, even if the stock market crashes, you have something real, something that will continue to appreciate in value. And even if that fails—if the market for Asian art completely dries up—if there's a nuclear war or something—well, then, you still have the Buddha, and you can learn non-attachment from it."

I've always had a hard time buying things. Anything. I grew up in a family where I was taught that anything bought simply for pleasure, for the sheer enjoyment of life, was a waste of money. Not a sin exactly—Jews don't really believe in sins—but an unforgivable self-indulgence, worthy of crippling guilt. There was always some distant, abstract "future" when I might need that money—as if the $1.50 I spent on a James Bond souvenir program would cripple my retirement fund.

The situation in my family was so bad, for so long, that only last year did my mother finally break down, go out to the store, and buy herself the one thing she has desperately desired since she was a little girl—and the one thing she didn't even pretend she could afford while my father was alive. This item wasn't a Buddha; almost the opposite. It was a mink coat.

Shopping itself, as we all know, can be a very liberating experience. It is a measure of our self-esteem that we allow ourselves to shop; a measure of even greater self-esteem if we shop for something expensive. In Western civilization, of course, this is taken even a step further, and the truly respected people are the ones who can spend money hand over fist on the utterly useless, or the wildly extravagant. My father was fond of saying that ours is the only society where people actually go out and spend three or four dollars a week for plastic bags to throw out their garbage in.

The point is that, aside from the value of a stable financial investment and the various spiritual benefits that might accrue from owning my very own Buddha, there was the liberating idea of *shopping* to get excited about. It was just what I needed to give this particular trip to Nepal a focus of sorts.

And at the end of it all—at the climactic moment, if I ever did find the Buddha of My Dreams—I would perform the ritual of "Letting Go" of a fairly large amount of money.

How much money? Good question. A hundred bucks might not buy me much, even in impoverished Nepal. No, this had to be brazen, wanton, cathartic. I would go all out, push my finances to the limit, and spend as much as $300 for a *flawless* little statue of the Buddha.

2

Every time I get off the plane in Kathmandu—right after climbing down the rollaway stairs and stepping onto the runway at Tribhuvan International Airport—I let out a whoop of jubilation. Something in the air is so immediately exotic, so full of the promise of liberation from the veneer of bullshit slopped onto my soul by Life in the Western World, that the moment of contact releases a shock of energy. I see it now as a kind of grounding: like touching a brass doorknob after shuffling around on a rug.

The very first time I went to Nepal, in the summer of 1979, I didn't actually whoop. The circumstances surrounding my arrival there were uniquely screwy. I had just spent three months in Greece, shoveling cement dust on a huge construction site on Crete in order to save up enough money to travel to Nepal and rendezvous with a beautiful American doctor I'd fallen in love with on one of the Aegean Isles. But you know how those things go. Two days before leaving Athens, I stopped in at the American Express office and picked up a letter stating that I would travel to Nepal at my own peril. Dorothy had fallen in love with another man.

Argh! I was crushed, but decided to go anyway. What the heck! Some kind of momentum was pulling me there, toward the foothills of the Himalayas; any decision to resist would have been futile—or even dangerous. Plus, my ticket was already paid for. Nonrefundable. It was off to Asia, or slink back home in disgrace.

I flew to Bombay, took a train to Patan, bought a ticket for the hourlong hop over the border, and landed in Kathmandu—a total unknown to me—on the morning of June 7, 1979. At lunch time—with no clues or preconceptions, nothing to go on but the smell of the air on that damp monsoon runway and a jarring, fifteen-minute taxi ride to the Kathmandu Guest House—I pulled out my journal and penned my first entry in the Kingdom of Nepal:

> This may be paradise, but it's too soon to tell. Soft raindrops from a sky free of humidity. In a corner of this gentle, flowered yard, a man with oak skin and a tattered rag of a shirt sets a pump into motion. Hungry, exhausted, deliciously alone. Welcome home. . . .

As things turned out, Dorothy and I were reunited and actually did fulfill our original fantasy of living together in Kathmandu for a while. Remembering those days, a line from John Updike comes to mind: "Reality is the running impoverishment of possibility." Somehow, her quick and dirty betrayal shattered the magic of the storybook infatuation that Dorothy and I had manufactured on the pheromone-buttered beaches of Greece. The romance sputtered and died. But sometimes these strange meetings and hellfire affairs are actually, we later discover, just catalysts for greater encounters. Dorothy introduced me not only to Nepal, but also to a rather singular character named Lalji, who I'll be mentioning later.

During that first trip to Nepal—which lasted five months—I shopped naively, buying a bunch of silly souvenirs and third-rate statues that have moldered in various attics around the San Francisco Bay area for the past decade, waiting for a cataclysmic earthquake to put them out of their misery. But there was more. I managed to write the first two hundred pages of a novel, based on my experiences working at that hellish construction site on Crete. At that point Kathmandu had but a single photocopying machine. The cost was so high (about 75 cents a page) that I had to make a choice: stay in Nepal another month or make a copy of my manuscript to mail home, in case something happened to the one I was carrying (or vice versa). In a fit of professional common sense, I chose the second option, and began to make my way back to the shiny shoes of Western civilization.

Realizing that I could write in Nepal (something I didn't seem to be able to do anywhere else), I wasted no time in engineering a way to get back there. My second trip to the kingdom began in the summer of 1983, when I received a generous twelve-month grant from the Rotary Foundation International to write what I had promised would be the "great Nepali-American novel." Instead I wrote lots and lots of letters, which ended up being compiled into a very different kind of book that I called *Mr. Raja's Neighborhood*. The novel was relegated to the back burner—where it has been bubbling and brewing in my brain, taunting and haunting me, ever since.

Toward the end of 1984, my grant money ran out (having been stretched, you can be sure, to the utter limit). I moved back to San Francisco and joined my friends in the desperate dog-paddle for economic survival that characterized the Reagan era. Ferreting with the industry of a truffle-hunting boar, I managed to drum up a more-or-less steady stream of interesting freelance writing jobs, exotic photography assignments, and irritating-but-well-paying PR stints. There was always an excuse to put off that novel, but what to say? You gotta make a living.

When I bought my ticket to go back to Nepal for the third time—in the summer of 1987—I had a particular agenda in mind.

To begin with, I had landed an assignment for *Mother Jones* magazine to write an investigative story about antiquities smuggling. This is a serious problem in Nepal; over the past few decades, somewhere between 30 to 50 percent of the kingdom's ancient art treasures have been stolen from their shrines and sold to dealers, collectors, and museums around the world.

The second part of my plan—which would actually come first, chronologically speaking—was to visit Tibet with my good friends Rick and Nancy. The three of us had met in Kathmandu in 1983; I was on my fellowship, and they were teaching English to high-school-aged Nepalis at the American Cultural Center. They lived in a Western-style, multilevel brick house in the Chhetrapati district of the city—a location that soon became famous for cutthroat weekend poker games (if you can call *rupee-ante* poker "cutthroat") followed by wanton dancing-'til-dawn to the tune of vintage Grateful Dead tapes.

I moved in with them in early 1984. We shared one of those perfect cohabitations that occurs maybe once every two or three lifetimes. I remember it as a constant stream of intelligent fun, punctuated by crippling stints of eye, nose, and throat infections, worms, amoebas, and boils. We took care of each other. We fell in love. Rick and Nancy moved back to Chicago and found a flat together; I returned to California alone. But the connection never loosened, and we ultimately decided to return to Asia and trek, as a threesome, through the mountains of Tibet.

Another motive for this third trip—not too loudly, please—was to try and make some headway on that novel I'd planned to write in 1983 and 1984. Maybe work on the outline, sketch out a chapter or two, develop a couple of characters. No commitments, no pressure, nothing to get neurotic about; oh no no no; just a little heat to keep that original inspiration, now over three years old, on a low simmer.

All the above is, of course, a gross simplification. There are deeper reasons to travel—itches and tickles on the underbelly of the unconscious mind. We go where we need to go, and then try to figure out what we're doing there. It took a surprisingly long time for me to realize that all these trips to Nepal and environs were united by a single, fundamental theme: the need to steep my cerebral cortex in the culture and religion of the region, in the hopes that as much of it would soak into me as possible.

It was like heaving my brain into a fathomless lake—an unpredictable pool that sometimes seemed as clear and clairvoyant as a crystal ball, but at other times rippled black and opaque, like octopus ink—and hoping it could swim.

The depth of the place! They call it the World's Only Hindu Kingdom, but that goes nowhere toward explaining the fantastic shades of animism, Hinduism, and Buddhism that have marbled, over the millennia, in the umbra of Earth's most mind-boggling mountain range. No one knows exactly how many gods and goddesses, how many saints, sages, and bodhisattvas are worshiped in Nepal. Nobody has lived long enough to make an accurate count of the benign and demonic deities who reside in the roaring peaks and glacial rivers, in the stones and trees, snakes and bumblebees. Mary Anderson, author of the indispensable *Festivals of Nepal*, writes that an old Hindu text puts the figure at an even 300 million—enough to assign every little girl in the kingdom (and every little boy, and all their friends and family) eighteen guardian deities all her own.

Hinduism (but let's call it Brahmanism, as savvy scholars prefer, since the word *Hindu* was a Western invention) was likely the wellspring of this fantastic pantheon. The source gods are Brahma, Vishnu, and Shiva: the Hindu trinity. It is from these three central figures that nearly all the countless others have taken form.

Despite the fact of these three main gods, and the added fact that each one of them has divided and subdivided into a cast of thousands of others, male and female, animal and monster; and despite the fact that each one of these gods and goddesses, no matter how obscure, holds some kind of final sway and is celebrated in a unique and individual way, devout Brahmans will clear their throats and remind you, Sir, that they are, bottom line, strictly monotheistic. All these other gods are themselves nothing but manifestations of The One. We speak now of Brahmana, the formless, all-powerful prime mover at dead center of all creation.

But omnipotent Brahmana is too fantastic and abstract to be comprehended by most mere mortals. Necessity demanded that, to facilitate worship, Brahmana be trisected into the three great protector deities.

There is Brahma, the supreme Creator, who formed the universe and all contained within it; there is Vishnu, the Great Preserver, who has the rather daunting job of protecting all that Lord Brahma has created; and there is Shiva, the potent Creator-Destroyer.

Lord Shiva, whose dreadlocked, trident-wielding devotees haunt the streets and temple grounds of Kathmandu, is god enough to keep any full-time worshiper busy for a lifetime. Among other attributes, Shiva is Lord of the Dance, Source of the Ganges, the Perfect Ascetic, and Protector of All Animals. Most important, Shiva is Time itself: supreme master of everything, both living and nonliving, that exists. It is Lord Shiva who commands the course of all matter, from conception and birth to death and dissolution. J. Robert Oppenheimer, builder of our first atomic bomb, reflected warily on his achievement with a quote from the Sanskrit: "I am become Shiva/Destroyer of Worlds."

Shiva's presence in the Kathmandu Valley—he keeps a little place by the Bagmati River—has indisputable side effects on Hindus and non-Hindus alike. If I were pressed to give one reason, one specific observation of why life in Nepal seems so much more vivid than life anywhere else, I would answer with a single word: *time*. There is a quality to time spent in Nepal that can only be described as *inhalant*.

Back home in the Wild West, time whips by with the relentless and terrible purpose of a strangling vine filmed in fast motion. A week, two months, ten years snap past like amnesia, a continual barrage of workdays, appointments, dinner dates and laundromats, television shows and video cassettes, parking meters, paydays, and phone calls.

You can watch it from Asia. You read the newspapers, you think about your friends back home—marching along in the parade of events—and you know it's still happening. It's happening *there*. On the other side. Yesterdays, todays, and tomorrows are tumbling after each other like Sambo and the tiger, blending into an opaque and viscous ooze. There is no such thing as *now*; only a continual succession of laters, whipping their tendrils around the calendar. The clutches of the vine. . . .

In Nepal, the phenomenon is reversed. Time is a stick of incense that burns without being consumed. One day can seem like a week; a week, like months. Mornings stretch out and crack their spines with the yogic impassivity of house cats. Afternoons bulge with a succulent ripeness, like fat peaches. There is time enough to do everything—write a letter, eat breakfast, read the paper, visit a shrine or two, listen to the birds, bicycle downtown, change money, buy postcards, shop for Buddhas—and arrive home in time for lunch.

Lord Shiva takes many forms: male and female, beastly and divine, compassionate and bloodthirsty. His main temple, golden-roofed Pashupatinath, lies just outside of Kathmandu, straddling the banks of the holy Bagmati River—which, flowing south to India, joins the Ganges. On the last full moon of each winter, the knolls and steps of Pashupatinath are carpeted with bong-smoking, glassy-eyed Shaivites who walk, ride, hitchhike and even crawl to Nepal from all over the subcontinent. They have come for Shivaratri, their master's annual festival, and their participation in this event often includes outrageous acts of self-mortification. One devotee, famous for his crazy piety, lops off a little bit more of his arm each year. . . .

As impressive a figure as Shiva is, the key to the Nepali equation is found elsewhere. It is held by Lord Vishnu: the Great Preserver, who single-handedly (actually, with twenty hands) unites the northern tides of Tibetan Buddhism with the southern swell of Brahmanism. Vishnu, the Nepalis believe, will be called on a grand total of ten times—awakened from his deep eternal snooze and pressed into action—in order to save the human race from extinction, the world from ruin, and the various realms of existence from a typhoon of chaos and calamity.

This has already occurred nine times. Vishnu's tenth avatar (as apocalyptic Jagannath, the rolling black chariot that destroys all in its path) will be his last.

Lord Vishnu's first six incarnations occurred so long ago that they are slowly settling into the silt of the collective unconscious. His seventh, eighth, and ninth, though, are still actively worshiped and respected throughout Asia, from the steaming deserts of Rajasthan in western India to the coconut-littered beaches of Thailand and Indonesia. They are literally the stuff of which best-sellers (as well as countless Hindi movies, stage dramas, and TV soap operas) are made.

For his seventh encore, Vishnu was born on Earth as a prince named Rama. His mission was to destroy a powerful, ten-headed demon named Ravana, who had succeeded in weaseling from the cowed gods a boon that rendered him invulnerable to both divine and beastly harm. Ravana hadn't bothered to take out a policy against humans; they were, after all, his preferred food. Rama, along with his brother Laxman and the monkey general Hanuman, laid waste to Ravana's plans of world domination. The story is told in what must be the world's most fantastic epic: the *Ramayana*.

In his eighth avatar, Vishnu appeared in the famous form known as Krishna: lover, flautist, and rascal extraordinaire. The epic *Mahabharata* tells the tale of that volatile era in human history. One particular chapter of that voluminous saga has achieved biblical status. The chapter, in which Krishna explains the rules governing the behavior of both human beings and gods, is known as the *Bhagavad-Gita*.

And the ninth? Aha. . . . For his ninth avatar, Vishnu, the Great Preserver, awakened, stifled a yawn, and set off once again to save the human race (this time from its own crazy foibles). This most recent visitation took place a mere 2,500 years ago. The form he chose was again both mortal and princely. His place of birth was in southern Nepal, in a peaceable kingdom called Kapilavastu.

At first, aside from his miraculous birth, there was nothing overwhelmingly remarkable about this precocious young prince of the Shakya clan. This all changed in 534 B.C. when, at the age of twenty-nine, tormented by the riddles of old age, disease, and death, Prince Siddhartha Gautama set off to find the antidote to human suffering. Six years later he succeeded and traveled off to teach what he had discovered

17

to anyone who might care to listen. Thus Vishnu's ninth incarnation became the historical personage known throughout the world simply as Buddha: the Awakened One.

This crucial keystone connecting Brahmanism and Buddhism partially explains the remarkable atmosphere of religious tolerance that prevails in Nepal (a tolerance that extends to the small Islamic community, though stumbling awkwardly over Christianity). Over the centuries, this broad-minded attitude has turned Nepal into a vast spiritual fermentation tank, where the sweetest artistic juices of Hinduism and Buddhism have run together like popsicles in a crucible. Buddhist and Hindu gods and goddesses rub shoulders at nearly every temple and in every celebration, strolling arm-in-arm down the broad avenues of myth.

It's the richest banquet imaginable. For anyone with an appetite for fantastic legends, a thirst for color (especially red), and a general craving for utter theological wonder, visiting Nepal is a case study in all-you-can-eat.

3

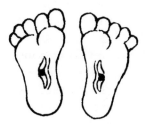

During my first visit to Nepal, it seemed to me that this soaking-up was a passive exercise—something that happened *to* you. Sure, I knew about the concept of *kharma:* of my good or evil words and deeds following me from one miserable lifetime to the next, until, at some point in the hazily distant future, the balance would at last be skewed in my favor and I would be ushered from this vale of tears and into the Clear Light. I just didn't figure there was much I could do about it, except behave myself and hope for the best.

Wrong. Dead wrong. . . . Sometime during my second trip, I caught on. In Asia, I learned, one can influence the inexorable tides of kharma far more efficiently than one can in the West. There is an ancient, time-honored tradition that allows you to earn what amount to spiritual Brownie points—to actively hedge your bets against coming back as a banana slug or pit bull—by undertaking certain labors. One may seek out blessings from lamas and yogis, perform pilgrimages to specific religious shrines, and/or visit any number of the countless sacred spots that cover the Asian landscape as thickly as a leopard's spots.

This process of collecting blessings is known as "acquiring merit." It is great fun and, for most of us, a very, very good idea.

These blessings can take many different forms. Certain lamas might hand out red strings or small amulets, which are tied around the neck. Others dispense tiny round pills, or sprinkle their devotees with holy water.

In more intimate circumstances, a lama or guru will share an especially effective breathing technique, or give a disciple a personalized *mantra*—a phrase filled with so much spiritual power that merely reciting it can help lift the devotee into a meditative trance state.

Maybe someday I would make that kind of connection and wind up the proud owner of a rare and precious mantra. But for the meantime, I was playing the peripatetic journalist—always on the go. All I wanted were the blessings themselves, and the tiny reassurance that I was keeping the tossing raft of my kharma on an even keel.

But that would take a lot of blessings. An endless river of them, I guessed. And so over the years, my desire to garner as many blessings as possible became an obsessive challenge, lying somewhere between a pious religious quest and hubcap collecting.

Predictably, this peculiarly Western approach to winning spiritual merit has its perils. One example in particular bears recounting.

While we were traveling in Tibet, Nancy, Rick, and I heard tales of an extraordinary, fifty-two-year-old woman who could perform miracles. Known as the Khandroma Rimpoche, she was believed to be the direct reincarnation of Lady Yeshe Tsogyal—consort of Padmasambhava, the legendary Indian mystic and sorcerer who brought Buddhism to Tibet in the eighth century A.D.

Khandroma Rimpoche, we'd heard, was one of the most enlightened and powerful women in Tibet. She had been known to fly through the air. On one occasion, during a storm, witnesses had seen her zoom to the top of a peak to catch a falling prayer flag pole before it touched the ground. Our minds boggled—what a coup it would be to get her blessing! But the quest for this prize would involve real work; the Khandroma Rimpoche lived with a few hearty attendants above an *ani gompa*, a magical nunnery hidden up a narrow, tortuous canyon, near the confluence of two mountain rivers.

The journey from Lhasa to the ani gompa, by bus, mule-drawn cart, and foot, took nearly a week. The final leg of our hike, through the cool and dripping canyon, seemed almost like a rebirth. Everything about that canyon—its smell, its temperature, the cries of its birds, and the marbled color of its walls—served to remind us that we were about to enter a world apart.

Emerging, we stood for a while above the ani gompa. Below, the two rivers collided in a roar of white foam. Rick passed some almonds and dried apricots around. Finally we heaved our packs back on and made the descent, entering the little nunnery-cum-village. Within a matter of minutes, the three of us found ourselves the sole guests of the nunnery's modest lodge.

Our hostess was a handsome *ani*, or nun. She was dressed in a heavy maroon-colored robe and wore a *malla* of 108 well-polished prayer beads wrapped around her forearm. As with all the nuns and monks we'd met, our ani's head had been recently tonsured. Her high, proud scalp was covered with the thinnest layer of hair, rising like the shoots of a newly planted lawn.

The ani watched with intense interest as we spread our down sleeping bags out on the narrow wooden cots and heaved our dusty backpacks onto the floor. The journey had been difficult, to say the least, and now that we had arrived at our destination it was only right and proper to reward ourselves. Rick cast me a conspiratorial glance and dug into his backpack for the waterproof sack containing our special, "treat" food.

While trekking in Tibet, we existed mainly on *tsampa*—finely ground barley flour that one mixes with salty, buttery tea to create a heavy porridge with the approximate appearance, aroma, and taste of fresh Play-Doh. One grows a bit weary of this fare. Anticipating this, we had brought various rations of our own: Quaker Oats instant cereal, bars of waxy Chinese chocolate, bags of nuts and raisins, and a bunch of Chinese army survival biscuits that looked like adobe bricks and were only slightly less dense than neutron stars.

There was one more food item, rare and precious, which we had decided beforehand to save for the most special occasion of our entire Tibetan sojourn. We had absolutely no hesitation in deciding that this moment—arriving at the doorstep of the remote and potent Khandroma Rimpoche—was it. With a solemnity bordering on the melodramatic, Rick located, displayed, and lovingly opened the single, priceless can of Starkist tuna fish, "packed in spring water," that we had carried to Tibet from a Safeway supermarket in Oakland, California. Every saliva duct in my mouth came alive as the nearly forgotten aroma of seafood wafted through the dirt-floored, stone-walled shack.

Within a split second, we had devoured the delicacy, a fact accomplished under the sharp and inscrutable eye of our portly hostess.

To say that our ani was hospitable would be the most banal of understatements. She was practically a Jewish mother. Less than an hour after our arrival she was already bringing us food: fresh Tibetan bread, hard cheese, and sour little apples. This gesture was repeated at dinnertime, and again the next morning. Our attempts to return the meals or con-

22

sume less than the full share she had brought were futile. The ani would sit down on one of the cots and watch us sternly, crying *"Sheh! Sheh! Sheh!"*—"Take! Take! Take!"—until the last bites disappeared from our plates.

It became embarrassing. We were uncomfortable—and a little bit puzzled—by the extent of this one-sided generosity. Tibet is by no means a bountiful land, and we couldn't help but feel that we must be imposing on our ani's frugal supplies.

Shortly after our arrival, we met another Westerner at the ani gompa. This was a tall, fair-skinned, clear-eyed woman called Ani Marilyn. Marilyn, a former Magnum photographer whose work had appeared, in the mid 1960s, in magazines ranging from *National Geographic* to *Vogue,* had "broken through" the glamorous life as an international photojournalist to pursue the austere Middle Way of Tibetan Buddhism. In 1987 she took full vows and was at last a fully ordained nun. Her Buddhist name was now Ngawang Chodron; but, as a kindness to those of us unaccustomed to speaking with the back of our throats, she consented to be called Ani Marilyn.

Since Ani Marilyn was fluent in Tibetan, we asked if she might intercede with our nun and discover the root of this obsessive desire to mother us. Marilyn agreed. A few hours later, she dropped by the visitors' lodge with an explanation.

"I spoke with your ani," Marilyn said. "She told me that right after you arrived, even though you must have been terribly hungry from your long journey, you had nothing to eat but a tiny, disgusting tin of dead fish. She has been going around the gompa, collecting food from the other anis in order to feed you properly. . . ."

After several blissful days at the gompa, we presumed to be on good enough terms with our ani to ask her an enormous favor. She listened to our pleas and finally consented, perhaps a bit apprehensively, to take us up the long, steep hillside that led to the Khandroma Rimpoche's secluded residence.

We were thrilled. We put on our best clothes and brought along fine silk *katas*—the traditional greeting scarves of the Tibetans—to present to this venerable woman. A kata is a marvelous thing; you offer one to a high lama, who blesses the scarf and places it around your neck. What better souvenir of our visit to the Khandroma Rimpoche than a fine silk kata, infused with the spiritual essence of Padmasambhava's closest consort?

Following our ani, who prayed and twirled her prayer wheel all the while, we finally arrived at the Khandroma Rimpoche's sanctuary. It was a stern domicile on a high ridge, commanding a tremendous view. We could see crumbling old retreat huts and shrines, crowning nearby peaks; prayer flags fluttering on high eyries; squat houses with *om*-carved stones cobbling their roofs.

Much to our dismay, though, the high lama herself did not turn out to greet us. The only people present were a few female caretakers. At first it looked like we would return totally empty-handed; but after a somewhat harsh exchange with our ani, one of them—a disheveled-looking woman with shoulder-length black hair and a grimy corduroy robe—consented to show us around. She brought us into a dank, dripping meditation cave and showed us a depression in the wall that was meant to be Padmasambhava's handprint. Then she pushed us rudely into kneeling position and ladled water from a cold, subterranean spring into our palms. We sipped it reluctantly, wary of microorganisms.

There was a pile of katas in a corner of the cave, but we were not about to toss our offerings onto that anonymous heap. Our supply of first-class katas was limited, and if we couldn't give our scarves to Khandroma Rimpoche herself, we figured we might just as well hang on to them for the next high lama.

So where was the Lady Yeshe Tsogyal, anyway? Now that the formalities of our little cave tour were over, we earnestly wished to meet her. We turned to our ani, who—knowing as little English as we knew Tibetan—was at a total loss to explain. She made some sort of cryptic, combing motion with her fingers, which seemed to indicate that the high lama was having her hair washed. The oldest excuse in the book!

Abruptly, our welcome expired. Our reluctant tour guide, visibly peeved, vanished from sight. Large was our disappointment as we were led back down the hill, still clutching our katas. It was impossible not to take the rejection personally. To make matters even more grim, the recently radiant sky was quickly filling with ill-omened clouds. Within an instant, we were caught in a cold deluge and soaked to the skin. I felt completely overwhelmed by dejection and misery.

Back at ani gompa, we ran immediately to Ani Marilyn and asked her to make sense of the encounter for us. What had gone wrong? Why had we been snubbed by the Khandroma Rimpoche? Was there any hope of seeing her in the future?

Ani Marilyn, the embodiment of patience, said she would find out what she could. She turned to our ani and had a long exchange, punctuated by incredulous looks and the hair-washing gesture that had so baffled us up at the Rimpoche's retreat. Finally, emitting a universal sigh of disbelief, Ani Marilyn turned back to us with three fatal words:

"That was her!"

Whaaaat . . . ?! That very woman—long-haired and clad in ragged robes—had been Yeshe Tsogyal herself! She had shown us the saint's palm print, blessed us with sacred water from Padmasambhava's own cave, and sent us on our way!

We were devastated—and it got even worse. We next learned that our own ani, our dear, generous ani, had been severely upbraided by the Rimpoche for invasion of privacy. That, Marilyn explained, was the essence of the angry exchange we had witnessed. Our hostess, so eager to please, had barged in on the highest lama in the region with a trio of nincompoops!

Rick and I listened to all this dumbly; but Nancy, pushed to the limit of shame and embarrassment, burst into tears. She ran from the lodge and stood outside the door as incredulous teenage anis, ruddy and wind-burned, ran up to surround her.

It was a miserable night, full of self-recriminations. Early the next morning we were awakened by our ani, who beckoned us to follow her. We were brought to Ani Marilyn's room. It was cold and damp, and we were completely puzzled, but Marilyn gave us each a cup of hot Tibetan tea and bid us wait. Several minutes later the curtain over the doorway was parted—and in walked Lady Yeshe! Word of our mortification—and especially of Nancy's astonishing tears—had reached the compassionate Khandroma Rimpoche, who descended from her hilltop eyrie to forgive us.

The Rimpoche stroked Nancy's tear-streaked cheeks, accepted our katas, and presented us with magical long-life pills. She then ran outside and returned in a split second carrying yet another gift: a huge cloth sack full of blessed barley flour and cheese, which she emptied, in its entirety, into three of our biggest Zip-lock bags! Yikes! Ten extra pounds of weight to carry! The food, which turned the plastic pouches into massive throw pillows, seemed equal parts punishment and gift—a "burden of nourishment" that was finally forced on us.

"Without speaking the same language," the Khandroma Rimpoche told us via Ani Marilyn, "we are nothing but animals." Her words rang painfully true. We had been little better than buffoons, bumbling about in search of abstract blessings from an enlightened woman whom we had failed to recognize—even when she was pouring holy water down our throats.

4

There was never any doubt that I wanted to buy a Buddha, first and foremost. That doesn't mean I wasn't willing to poke around for other deities; by this point, having convinced myself that Nepalese art was both a sound investment and a useful tool for self-improvement, I entertained the thought of going home with as many sculptures as I could possibly carry.

So, while combing through Kathmandu's seemingly endless array of galleries, shops, and street stalls in search of the perfect Buddha, I took ample time to acquaint myself with some of the other popular gods and goddesses who fill out the ranks of what I, irreversibly conditioned by years of Hebrew school, must very respectfully refer to as the Lower Arcana. Because as much as I loved them, and as irresistibly as I was drawn to worship them, these other characters are not merely enlightened gurus, but full-fledged *gods*. Idols! Graven images! The closer I got to them, the closer I skirted to the steep and guilty edges of the Golden Calf syndrome: a common affliction among Jews in Asia.

But after all was said and done, nothing in the world could keep me from admiring, appraising and, yes, embracing these imaginative, voluptuous deities. And hey—why not? I mean, what business is it of mine if God decides to take one, ten, or thirty million forms? Who am I to reject these divine manifestations of the Eternal, anyway? Nobody! Nothing! A mote! Better by far, I reasoned, to follow the old "when in Rome" wisdom and throw myself whole hog into the arms of that luscious, though decidedly nonkosher, pantheon.

Tara, a goddess of compassion, is a lovely sight—her full, perfectly molded breasts garlanded with flowers, her hips subtly bent, her delicate right foot resting on a blossoming lotus. . . . And yet, sighing with decidedly nonreligious longing, I couldn't help but wonder if I could be accused of ulterior motives for buying a statue that looked as if it belonged on the beach at St. Tropez.

A friend of mine who lives and works in Kathmandu made that very mistake; he bought a gorgeous standing Tara at one of the shops outside of Bodhnath Temple, brought it home, and put it in his bedroom. After a few weeks he began to realize that he was becoming obsessed, unable to romance a real flesh-and-blood woman while this slender embodiment of compassion watched from the foot of the bed. He ultimately had to move his Tara into the living room and drape a sheet over the statue when expecting female company.

But how about Ganesh? Ganesh is irresistible, with his big fat belly and Babar the Elephant's head. Ganesh is the god of auspicious beginnings, and one of the most popular gods in Asia. All I could think of the first time I saw him was the Flying Dumbo ride at Disneyland, a passage that remains my very earliest memory from childhood.

Lord Ganesh is the son of Shiva, the great god of Destruction in the Hindu trinity, and of Parvati, Shiva's delicious consort. The story behind the elephant's head varies in details from place to place, but the general scene was this:

One day Parvati, taking a leisurely bath, decides that she wants a son, someone who will answer to her and her alone. She scrubs down her skin, collecting together a large lump of saffron, and fashions from this fragrant mass a boy. The moment he attains consciousness, Parvati names him Ganesh and puts him to work. She orders him to stand guard by the palace door, and to let no one—absolutely no one—enter.

Shiva, naturally, picks this precise moment to return home from some messy mythical altercation. Our hero is, understandably, rather single-minded in his desire to frolic with lovely Parvati. Seeing this strange child haughtily blocking the door, Shiva demands to be admitted. Ganesh flatly refuses.

Some say the battle was long; others claim it lasted only an instant. It ended, at any rate, with Ganesh's head lying on the ground, a fair distance from the rest of his body. This accomplished, Shiva strolled into the parlor, but the homecoming wasn't quite what he had anticipated. Parvati was furious, and all thoughts of romance were tabled until Shiva somehow put the situation to rights. Desperate to appease his wife, Shiva raced out and appropriated the head of the first animal he saw: a baby elephant. After the successful transplant, Shiva further sweetened the pot by granting his son special privileges, including extraordinary intelligence and a high status among his fellow gods.

Ah, Ganesh! Remover of obstacles, protector of children and thieves, patron of the poets! Ages ago, when the great sage Vyasa was suddenly struck by the inspiration to dictate the monumental epic *Mahabharata* in one sitting, Ganesh volunteered to serve as scribe. Halfway through Vyasa's feverish and unflagging dictation, the pen burst into flame and disintegrated. Ganesh, fearful of missing even a single syllable, snapped off his own tusk to use as a quill. Peerless devotion to the art! What better ally, I ask you, for a writer whose pen is perpetually out of steam? What more loyal mascot than this holy Dumbo incarnation?

Or how about the bodhisattva Manjushri? Manjushri, Embodiment of Wisdom, whose pure and peerless incisiveness is symbolized by a flaming sword, held high?

Manjushri is one of the patron deities of Kathmandu. The story goes like this: thousands of years ago, he visited the valley, which was then a huge lake with a miraculous flaming lotus shimmering on its surface. Manjushri had come to meditate on the edge of the holy lake and contemplate the mystery of its famous flame. After he had done so for a while he rose to his feet, stretched his legs, and began to walk around the entire periphery of the lake. He did this three times before pausing at the southern rim. There Manjushri drew his magical sword and swung it above his head, bringing it down with devastating force into the hill beside him. There was a thunderous roar as the earth split, creating the deep rift known today as Chobar Gorge.

The waters rushed out through the gap. Within a few weeks, the Kathmandu Valley lay drained and tender beneath the sun—sacred ground from Day One. Humans arrived shortly thereafter.

What can compete with so potent a metaphor? I must admit that at first, before I thought I was really good enough to own my own Buddha, it seemed that Manjushri alone might be enough to satisfy my gnawing appetite for an all-purpose icon.

But no. I wanted it all. I mean, if I was prepared to spend a couple of hundred dollars for one of these gods I wanted as much for my money as possible. Wisdom. Compassion. Protection. Peace of mind! And for sheer devotional value, ounce for ounce, nothing beats a Buddha.

31

A Buddha is not a simple thing to shop for. He comes in infinite sizes, a full spectrum of colors, and a daunting variety of postures and poses. The postures—standing, walking, reclining, or sitting in meditative bliss—are called *asanas*. Then, to complicate matters even further, there are the *mudras:* hand positions. Sometimes the Buddha's fingers are intricately linked in the tongue-wrestling pose of *dharmachakrapravartanamudra:* "Turning the Wheel of the Law." Or with his right palm raised: "Fear Not." Both hands up, palms facing outward: "Calming the Ocean." Once, at a temple in Thailand, I think I saw a gesture called "Forbidding His Relatives to Fight with One Another."

Fortunately, I knew from the very beginning which *asana* and *mudra* I wanted. The pose is sometimes called "Subduing Mara"; but the more familiar title, which I prefer, is *bhumisparsamudra:* "Calling the Earth to Witness."

That pose seemed to embody the state of mind that would fix me up once and for all—it spoke of an approach to life and to work that I needed to be reminded of constantly.

Why? Well, I think it has to do with an unconscious fear of success: a very contemporary (and peculiarly American) malaise that, much like chronic fatigue syndrome, you never even realize exists until your lover or your analyst uses it to explain what's been wrong with you all these years. Then the indisputable accuracy of the diagnosis washes over you like a hot tide, your face burns with the sugar rush of catharsis, and you are filled with the giddy conviction that you can make it all happen after all.

And why not? I mean, if the problem is fear of success, and you can somehow eliminate the fear, then all that's left is success: gleaming out there on the horizon like an illuminated skyline, brilliant, inevitable, you couldn't miss it if you tried.

So why not another pose, like "Fear Not"? Well, if the only thing to fear was fear itself, then that "Fear Not" pose might be enough. But this is not just plain, ordinary fear of something like death, or rotten shellfish. This is fear of *success*, a far more insidious foe. It elbows its way into every situation, from table tennis to romance, and takes many strange and terrible forms—not the least of which, as any writer knows, is a relentless, demonic distraction.

On the surface, this distraction may manifest as a simple desire for a pepperoni pizza or cup of espresso. You know the technique: momentary diversion. What the demon *really* wants to do, of course, is snatch the page right out of my typewriter carriage, read it with a sneer, and howl, "This really *stinks*, boy! It's the worst kind of amateur drivel! What makes you think you can get away with inflicting this gibberish on anyone with brains enough to avoid it? What gives you the *right*?"

Buddha did not suffer from fear of success. He was one of those rare characters, like Joan of Arc or Lawrence of Arabia or Pablo Picasso, who know beyond a shadow of a doubt that their lives hold a particular destiny. For people like this, life is just a matter of waiting, patiently, for the appropriate moment to come before stepping, in sandals or boxer shorts, into the mythos.

Prince Siddhartha Gautama was twenty-nine years old when he vanished from his father's plush castle at Kapilavastu—near what is now Lumbini, in southern Nepal—and set off to find the "deathless state." He drifted from one great mystic and teacher to another—trying first yoga, then seclusion, then torturous self-denial. None of these devices satisfied him for more than a year or two. The problem wasn't Siddhartha's attention span; he simply mastered each new school of thought and moved on to the next curriculum, until every available doctrine had been tested—and rejected.

So Siddhartha Gautama placed himself beneath a tree and vowed to remain there, empty-headed and motionless, until he arrived at the place called enlightenment.

After seven weeks, he was close—very, very close. So close that it was just a matter of saying yes. But just as he sat there, motionless beneath that famous Bodhi tree, just as he drew in his breath for that one simple monosyllable, who should appear out of nowhere but Mara, Lord of the Underworld, who tipped his Stetson hat, adjusted his mirror sunglasses, and approached the tree beneath which the would-be Buddha now sat.

And Mara said, "Hey, good work! Congratulations! Listen, I can tell when a man needs a drink; have a whiskey sour!"

And the Buddha said, "I don't drink!"

And Mara said, "Just one, c'mon, it's on me."

And the Buddha said, "No, thanks!"

And Mara said, "Well, then, have a cookie!"

And the Buddha said, "No, thanks!"

And Mara said, "Oh yeah?" and summoned together his irresistibly beautiful daughters. And these girls danced for the Buddha in their *Sports Illustrated* bathing suits and slowly wriggled out of even those velveteen leopard-skin Neoprene suits. . . . And if you have a hard enough time keeping your eyes in your head while strolling down the streets in a Great American City on a warm spring day when you feel good-lookin' and sexy and powerful, just imagine the pitiless predatory pheromones saturating that quiet grove 2,500 years ago, as Buddha sat there, possibly with a huge and final erection, and Mara's daughters ran their long brown hands over their smooth bodies with shivers of damp anticipation.

And Buddha said, "No, thanks!"

Then Mara pulled out his own pornography collection: big colorful full-page spreads advertising Froot Loops and shiny cars with all the options; laptop computers and flavored Chapstick and really comfortable sheepskin boots; violent cartoons and gory thrilling special effects and horrible traffic accidents, the dirtiest parts of a thousand hot books condensed into one word, incredibly realistic images of Siddhartha as a rock n' roll star and astronaut and best-selling author.

And Mara said, "All this and more, baby. C'mon, we love ya'. Have a drink!"

And the Buddha said, "No, thanks!"

Mara could only sputter and gape at this individual. Finally, he nodded his head.

"Okay," he drawled, "Okay. So you can't be tempted. Well, bully for you. Just one last question, though. What I wanna know is this: who gives you license to sit here and decide that what you know, what you think you know, is worth hearing, let alone worth teaching? Where do you get off, claiming that you could be the Enlightened One? What gives you the *right?*"

Siddhartha reached down with his right hand and lightly touched the earth. There was a stillness in the grove, and Mara could see the eyes staring at him from all directions. Bird eyes, rabbit eyes, snake eyes, mole eyes, bug eyes, tree eyes, stone eyes, all peering at him, surrounding the Buddha, and the wind through the trees whistling

"Weeeeeeeeeeeeeeeeeeeeeeeeeeeeeeeeeeeeeeeeeeeeeeee. . . ."

That pose: Buddha in full lotus, his left hand resting in his lap, untrembling. Fingers of the right hand gently grazing the ground. That was the pose I wanted.

Maybe someday, whilst toiling away, tottering on a wobbling log above the quicksand of deadlines and anxiety, teeth gnawing at my fingernails, flat down busted at the eternal beginning, or mired in the middle of things, thinking, "Help! Help! Anything but this! Jeez, I know, maybe I'll just get up and fix myself a nice whiskey sour, or grab some cookies real quick from the corner store, or, hey, why not give sweet Susie Swimsuit a call. . . ."

At that very moment a calm, confident voice, seeming to originate from the shelf above my printer, will murmur,

"No, thanks!"

And I'll look up to see those half-closed eyes; that gentle understanding smile; that light, light, light touch on the earth—and I'll know better.

This form of yours, calm yet lovely, brilliant without
dazzling,
Soft but mighty,—whom would it not entrance?
Whether one has seen it a hundred times, or beholds it
for the first time,
Your form gives the same pleasure to the eye.
             —CONZE et al., *Buddhist Texts Through the Ages*

So what does one look for in a statue of the Buddha? What
makes a work of figurative art a Buddha and not, say, a Ram-
bo doll or a clay bust of Elvis?

According to Matricheta, an Indian poet who lived four-
teen centuries ago, the figure of a Buddha "blazes with im-
mutable signs and marks." You can't miss him; in a world
populated by billboards and "Beware of Dog" signs he stands
out as radiant and unmistakable as a theater marquee: *Gone
With the Wind.* The people of ancient India, in fact, went so
far as to catalog the thirty-two major (and eighty minor!)
traits that positively identify a Buddha. For the purposes of
this exercise, though, this crash course in Buddha hunting,
we will content ourselves with enumerating only seven-
teen—a nice, prime number—of the most obvious and interesting protrusions and coruscations:

- Buddha's feet are often marked with wheels. This symbolizes the sacred duty of a *chakravartin*, or Universal Monarch: to Turn the Wheel, and keep it turning. Prince Siddhartha himself, after his enlightenment, began to travel far and wide to spread his teachings, which he claimed were based on neither faith nor magic but on a foundation of sound logic: the inevitable chain of birth, existence, and death. In doing this, it is said that the Buddha "turned the wheel of the law."

- Buddha's palms, meanwhile, should bear the signs of the lotus blossom and the conch shell trumpet.

- His earlobes, always pierced, are long and pendant, hanging down almost to his shoulders: a sign of noble birth (or, at least, weighty earrings).

- Buddha's hair is formed in kinky little curls, each of which turns clockwise. The curls look like snails; and some say that's just what they are. One afternoon, as the shorn Siddhartha meditated in the broiling Indian heat, an entire tribe of the mollusks noticed that the unshaded saint was in grave danger of stroke. Rushing to the scene—as best as they could, being snails—they completely covered his bald scalp to protect him from the blazing sun.

- A bump, called the *ushnisha*, is added to his cranium. This mysterious lump, never satisfactorily explained, might be a visual metaphor for the source of Buddha's wisdom. Another, stranger interpretation is that the image is accurate; that Siddhartha's head was actually a different shape from our own, containing an entirely new, enlarged, and improved brain. Personally, I think that idea is subversive. One of Buddhism's central concepts is that anyone can aspire to buddhahood, given purity of heart and discipline of mind. You don't have to grow another head first. At least, not literally.

- A molelike *urna* appears between his eyebrows. Some say it represents the all-seeing Third Eye. For others, the *urna* itself is a source of light.

- Buddha's eyes are centered and slightly downcast; neither truly open nor truly closed; neither focused nor unfocused. It's a look of both absolute detachment and perfect awareness. There is nothing in a Buddha's expression more important than the cast of those eyes. They should draw you in, but without seduction; they should hold you but not by capture. The perfect Buddha eyes are perfectly ambiguous. Sometimes they seem directed completely inward, opaque as moonstones; but sometimes, deep in meditation, you glance up and see them looking right at you: those penetrating open eyes, fully encouraging, slightly amused, eternally patient.

- The Buddha image is designed according to strict canonical formulas, exactly proportioned so that each eye, each nipple, every finger, urna and ushnisha alike, all balance in precise and perfect relation and proportion to every other part.

- The Buddha's lower neck is encircled by three rings, like the "mouth" of a conch shell.

- He has feet with level tread.

- The Buddha has long, sensuous fingers and toes; he does not crack his knuckles or bite his nails.

- It has been said that Buddha was seven feet tall, and that his proportions mirrored those of the banyan tree: that the height of his body should equal the length of his two arms when fully extended.

- For those of you who have passed muster on all the signs and marks so far, here is another simple test: a Buddha can touch his knees with his hands while standing erect.

- His skin is the color of gold.

- His form is consistently rounded. One thinks of Picasso's concept of the perfect human sculpture: water poured over the head should flow down to cover every other part of the body.

- Buddha's shoulders are as broad as a lion's.

- The Buddha is always clothed in the simple, traditional robes of a monk. This aspect of the Buddha image tends to change, across Asia, depending on the styles that have evolved in each particular land.

One of the first things required of me in my search for a man-made deity was that I become conversant with all these distinguishing marks; the signs and symbols that help people recognize Buddha when he comes strolling up to their picnic. I soon discovered, puttering about in my research, that Buddha himself—the historical Buddha, portrayed in countless statues—doesn't have a monopoly on divine deformities. Many of these same marks and signs, subtly (or not so subtly) varied, are shared by other Buddha-like beings known as *bodhisattvas.*

The concept of bodhisattvas is one of the central ideas of *Mahayana,* or "Greater Vehicle" Buddhism, which evolved around the beginning of the Christian era and took firm hold in countries such as Nepal, Tibet, Mongolia, China, and Japan. Before Mahayana, enlightenment was more or less a selfish concept; you were in it for yourself. Buddha was worshiped, as were the *arhats* who had been his direct disciples, and that was about as far as it went.

The Mahayanists felt that this approach had grown a little bit stale. Their conviction was deeply underscored by the sobering fact that Hinduism was beginning to make a major comeback in areas that had previously been converted to

Buddhism. So they went to work, developing a whole new Buddhist literature and style. Their manifesto included the concept that compassion, as an end in itself, was a key qualification for buddhahood—right up there with personal wisdom, so highly valued by the newly (and pointedly) coined *Hinayana* ("Lesser Vehicle") Buddhists. As a result of this more liberal view, the Mahayana iconography mushroomed to embrace not just the usual run of disciples and saints, but other perfectly evolved, perfectly compassionate, and—more to the point—nonmythical human beings as well.

To explain the marvelous, almost superhuman state of wisdom and compassion apparent in certain lamas, teachers, and legendary mystics, the Mahayanists developed the concept of bodhisattvas. A bodhisattva is a being who has, in a previous lifetime, attained the enlightened level of buddhahood, but who has mindfully refused the delightful rewards of *nirvana* (literally, extinction)—choosing, instead, to be reborn on the earth and to lend a hand until all other sentient beings are liberated as well.

A bodhisattva is a person who has dedicated an entire lifetime to perfecting the ultimate cheesecake, delicious, creamy, melt-in-your-mouth cheesecake, until finally God on high is compelled to take notice. And God says, "You have pleased me with your efforts. Try this cheesecake; *I baked it Myself.*" And the bodhisattva bows deeply, takes God's very own cheesecake, and carries it to the park as an offering to the homeless and the insects.

The realization that certain beings could keep coming back, again and again and again, set me off on a bizarre tangent. . . .

I've heard it said that the age of heroes is over. Certainly, there doesn't seem to be a heroic disposition in most people's minds. No wonder, when you take a look at our fearless leaders.

Still, I sometimes suspect that the problem isn't a lack of heroes so much as a flaw with the word itself. *Hero*. It seems obsolete, metallic, and unapologetically macho, conjuring up images of warriors, quarterbacks, astronauts, firemen, and the whole musty pantheon of Greek and Roman mythology. The so-called heroes touted in the U.S. media are usually politicians, captains of industry, or garden-variety humans who have performed a single act of great courage, perhaps accidentally, before fading out of the airwaves and back into the urban sprawl.

Joseph Campbell, the great mythologist who wrote *The Hero with a Thousand Faces*, tried to breathe new life into the term. He acknowledged the classic idea that a hero is someone who performs an amazing deed, but also defined heroes as adventurers: individuals who "learn to experience the supernormal range of human spiritual life" and then return to share their message with humanity. Campbell's was a valiant effort, but couldn't really undo all the itchy connotations that word has picked up on its own journey across the centuries. I'm inclined to believe that the majority of Americans who hear the word still think primarily of John F. Kennedy, Billie Jean King, or Superman.

Forget about heroes. The ones we want to watch for now are the bodhisattvas. These are the mindful and mysterious men, women, and children who seem to recognize, almost from Day One, their peculiar function on this planet. These people aren't flashes in some heroic pan; they've signed on for the whole menu. They are indeed adventurers; and the terrain they navigate reaches across all levels of human experience, from the cancer ward to the recording studio.

Recognizing them isn't always easy. Their urnas and ushnishas have been corrected with skillful surgery, the rings around the neck concealed with scarfs or collars, the eyes raised level, the wardrobes expanded. But there are always clues, giveaways, by which these great compassionate beings reveal themselves to us.

And there are so many of them! We all know a few, public and private. From the schoolyard to the spa, we've all met examples of these undercover deities, conspiring, through whatever means necessary and using the very tools of Western civilization, to lift our cerebral butts out of the gutter.

Who qualifies? How long does it take one of your garden-variety bodhisattvas to recognize what she or he is? Am I one? Are you? Would we know it if we were?

Alas: there is no test. There is no model. There are no answers. But please consider, merely for the sake of argument, the following cases:

Vincent van Gogh, preacher in the coal mines, lover of street whores, epileptic Dutch mahatma, reeling drunk on the sweet, wheat-scented oxygen of this mad, spinning planet he raged and painted. . . .

Woody Allen, jazz clarinetist and perfect Fool, provoking our laughter in the face of *samsara*—that big busy running-wheel of life, death, and human suffering upon which we are all hapless hamsters. "I don't want to achieve immortality through my work; I want to achieve it through not dying."

Mother Teresa, for deciding on the spur of an instant to be the conscience of the entire human race. . . .

Pablo Picasso, earnest clown and animal lover, yet perhaps the only bodhisattva capable of sitting through a bullfight; reborn on this Earth in order to keep artists from taking themselves too seriously. . . .

Martin Luther King, Jr., last best hope of a generation that now seems distant indeed; a man blessed with great wisdom, compassion, and the courage to bring these into the savaged streets. . . .

Ben Cartwright, *Bonanza's* wise and compassionate father figure, reminder of the days when heroes carried guns just to prove they didn't have to use them. . . .

Helen Keller, bodhisattva of humanity's blind trapped soul, smiling with pure inner light in every photograph. And wasn't Anne Sullivan, Miracle Worker, a bodhisattva as well?

Tenzig Gyatso, the Fourteenth Dalai Lama of Tibet, who is believed to be a direct reincarnation of Chenrezig, the bodhisattva of compassion. Throughout his long exile, and in the face of countless atrocities committed against the Tibetan people, he has remained our best example of Buddha-nature at its inventive best.

Thomas Edison, inventor extraordinary, master of *vajrayana*, the lightning path; who gave us film and music and so opened our eyes and ears to the plights and delights of sentient beings everywhere. . . .

Anne Frank (and the family who hid her!), for the awful, poignant metaphor of her life—and her lonely, classic sutra on suffering. . . .

Alexander Calder, delighted comic sculptor, who taught art how to dance. . . .

Arthur C. Clarke, writer and scientist, who invented the greatest tool of this century—the communications satellite—and refused to patent it, claiming that it should belong to all humanity. . . .

Satchmo Armstrong, bodhisattva, humble lusty monk with trumpet bell begging bowl: "Early in life I set myself out to be a happy man, and made it."

John Lennon, Josephine Baker, and Mahatma Gandhi; Ram Dass, Anaïs Nin, and Jonas Salk; Sir Edmund Hillary,

Saint Joan, Pandit Ravi Shankar; Mikhail Gorbachev, Walter Cronkite, Mr. Rogers. . . . How can we list them all? How can we possibly recognize the whole lot of them? The ones who have risen to fame; the ones forever lost in obscurity; the moms and dads and water carriers, translators and teachers and hermits, those exalted into the pages of *People* magazine or buried, fully content, in simple lives of service. . . .

Bodhisattvas known and unknown walk the earth, large and small, young and old, knowing or naive, but all brought to us through the same, ultimate sacrifice: by having agreed, in spite of temptations we can barely comprehend and could never resist, to be reborn on this insane planet one more time, full of their egos and their afflictions, their inflamed tonsils and itching hemorrhoids, to bring some tiny measure of knowledge or compassion to the plaintive, bewildered inhabitants of Earth.

6

Now that I knew precisely what I was after, at least as far as Buddha statues were concerned, the next step was finding it. This proved to be just a shade more difficult than I had imagined; despite the fact that in Kathmandu—as well as in the neighboring village of Patan, famed for its ancient tradition of metal casting—whole districts of "curio" shops offer on-sale deities. Tara and Ganesh and Manjushri, Durga and Shiva and Padmasambhava, an all-star cast of wrathful, compassionate, voluptuous gods and goddesses gleam behind warping panes of cheap Indian glass.

I embarked upon these adventures in shopping in the company of Nancy, the friend with whom I had recently traveled in Tibet. Known for her infectiously buoyant personality, Nancy had recently joined the ranks of the walking wounded. She had fallen in love (or "merged," to use her favored phrase) with an exquisite statue of the goddess Tara. The Tara had been one-of-a-kind, breathtakingly beautiful, but a bit beyond her means. Nancy had deliberated and, all but convinced, decided to sleep on it. Unfortunately, a somewhat more experienced buyer entered the shop a few moments after she left. Nancy rushed back first thing the next morning, bristling with those natural amphetamines that permeate the bloodstream just before a large and important purchase—only to discover that her Tara had just been given a one-way ticket to Düsseldorf.

This crushing disappointment colored, to an alarming extent, the way that Nancy and I went about our rounds. There was a need for non-attachment, to be sure; but also a prerequisite of knife-like resolve. It was as if, here in this distant, exotic land, we were compelled to raise the art of shopping to an experience that was, on the one hand, detached and almost Zen—our ultimate goal was, after all, enlightenment—and on the other hand, tinged with desperation, like shopping at Macy's or Bloomingdale's during a one-day-only White Sale: viciously predatory, and laced with the fear that the choicest Buddhas would be gone, snatched up if we hesitated too long, or neglected to visit each and every shop the very day that new work was due to arrive. Because, in spite of the deceptively vast quantity of statues displayed in the windows and on tattered blankets covering the sidewalks outside of the major hotels, most are chintzy rubbish; the ill-conceived abominations of a tourist-trap industry.

Some archetypes! If these were real humanoids, they'd be barred from military service: club-footed, triple-jointed, bug-eyed, eleven-toed, elephant-eared abominations with monkey-long limbs ending in pawlike appendages, with bronze or copper flashing festering like mold under the armpits: the kind of thing you wouldn't even want to use as a paperweight. Some were so ill proportioned, they flew so hard in the face of anatomy, that I had to wonder if the artists had ever seen a human being before. The statues reminded me of those old European drawings of elephants and rhinoceroses, based on distant sightings or wild rumor.

And then there were the copies. Back in 1984, when I was shopping for my first Ganesh, I found a very handsome one copied from a statue in the National Museum. By now, though, all those first-generation duplicates had been sold. The copies made from the copies were also gone; as were the copies made from the copies made from the copies. And with each consecutive recasting, you can be very sure that something had been lost in the translation.

For example: imagine taking an original Rembrandt drawing, and photocopying it on a primitive machine. You now put the flawed copy back on the glass, copy that, and repeat the whole process another three or four times. Come the fifth generation, you're holding something that looks more like a Franz Kline than a Dutch Master. Likewise, by the time Nancy and I encountered them, the 1987 model Buddhas were little more than crude lumps of bronze heaped into vaguely recognizable postures. Their feet and fingers exhibited the terminal stage of leprosy, while the faces—those all important, so-serene Buddha faces—looked like they'd just gone twelve rounds with Jake LaMotta.

But I'm making it all sound like a hopeless quest, and that's nowhere near the truth. Because every so often, in one of maybe three or four very exclusive shops—and not in the front foyer, but concealed in musty back rooms—we would discover a statue that made me sigh with a feline growl of primal longing. These were statues that crossed the Pygmalion line and seemed fully infused with life.

Half-closed eyes, perfectly centered, and just a hair downcast; the corners of the mouth curving up, so, so subtly, into what might be a smile. That smile is more than an invitation; it's the whole party.

Those statues are few and far between, hidden in drawers and cupboards, wrapped in rice paper and string, but always outlandishly expensive, and reserved for some Japanese or German buyer. We were lucky enough to even *see* them; the mere knowledge that these statues existed, that the Nepalis still created objects with this much grace and power, was a truth reserved only for the most persistent, impulsive collectors: people who would *kill* for a really good Buddha.

And so it got to the point where we shopped with consummate single-mindedness of purpose. We would look only at the best. Often we would enter a shop and, barely glancing at the inferior products on the shelves, demand instantly to be taken into the back room to see the newest, the latest, the most expensive work. We were the elite; the ones who knew the veins and arteries of the business. We were connoisseurs of Buddhas, of Taras, of Manjushris; and we begged not to be insulted by clumsy or sloppy workmanship.

And here I beheld the first of many twisted Zen truths pretzeled throughout this crazy koan called Shopping for Buddhas: only through the yoga of true pushiness, only by being relentlessly pushy in the most charming possible way, would I ever find the prize that I was seeking: a Buddha that really said something; or, a Buddha that really said *nothing*— and said it loudly enough for me to hear.

7

Suppose a man were pierced with a poisoned arrow, and his friends and relatives got together to call a surgeon to have the arrow pulled out and the wound treated.
If the wounded man objects, saying, "wait a little. Before you pull it out, I want to know who shot this arrow. Was it a man or a woman? Was it someone of noble birth, or a peasant? What was the bow made of? Was it a big bow or a small bow? Was it made of wood or bamboo? And what was the bow string made of? Fiber, or gut? Before you extract the arrow, I want to know all about these things."
Before all this information can be secured, no doubt, the poison will have time to circulate all through the system and the man may die. The first duty is to remove the arrow, and stop its poison from spreading.
In the search for truth there are certain questions that are unimportant. If a person were to postpone his searching and practice for enlightenment until such questions are solved, he would die before he found the path.
—BUKKYO DENDO KYOKAI, *The Teaching of Buddha*

It was at just about this juncture in time that I began to see everything that had transpired over the past few months—from the encounters with the Khandroma Rimpoche in Tibet to the hair-raising hike from Gosainkund Lake and the wanton marketplace madness that followed—as elements of a strange and inscrutable whole. My headlong search for a perfect Buddha suddenly took on bold new dimensions. It began to seem less like an unbridled shopping spree and mushroomed in my imagination into an epic quest, an odyssey capable of embracing nearly every situation I had ever encountered in Nepal or Tibet.

With this in mind, and inspired by recollections of Gurdjieff, I found myself recalling the single most remarkable man that I have ever met during my trips to Asia. He is a sort of haywire mystic, just a few years older than myself. It had been he, I think, who got my interest in Eastern thought rolling; for it had been he who first grabbed and twisted, a good decade earlier, the deeply lodged arrow tipped with my peculiar poison.

During my first visit to Nepal in 1979, Dorothy—the woman I had followed, in ill-fated pursuit, from Greece—developed a somewhat irritating relationship with a self-styled guru named Lalji. Every afternoon she would return from his house (he owned a bunch of chicken coops near the Bagmati River) and expostulate, Moonie-fashion, on all the marvelously insightful things he had said to her.

I was fresh from college at the time—B.A. in psych, *magna cum laude*—and had very little patience for the way this guy was spilling out all these great truths about Dorothy's past, present, and future. There was only one cure for my skepticism, Dorothy said. I would have to meet him. So one afternoon we cycled along Kalimati Road and forked left, down a muddy track that led to his compound.

Lalji greeted us by his gate, dressed in a bright pink sweatshirt. He was trim, if not athletic, with a round head and prominent ears. His black eyes danced, and as he gave me the once-over I thought I detected the eager, gleeful expression of a biology whiz kid who is about to pith and dissect his first frog.

Basically, I had been invited to observe a session between himself and Dorothy. I listened attentively, albeit suspiciously, to everything he said, cutting in now and again to chuckle, shake my head, and offer up bits of wisdom from the venerable *science* of psychology. Whenever I did so, I noticed Lalji peering at me with a kind of grudging admiration, like a magician who becomes aware that someone in the audience has figured out his tricks.

When it came time to go I felt well satisfied, secure in the knowledge that I'd given Lalji, if not a formal come-uppance, an indication that at least one person saw him for what he was: another Hindu fakir, stropping his spiritual razors on the Western money belt.

After we left his place, as Dorothy and I were walking down the little dirt path that led along the river and away from Lalji's compound, we heard the gate creak open, and Lalji's voice call to us from behind.

"Dorothy! Dorothy!" He was leaning out of his front yard and shouting in an agitated manner. "This is very important! Please, please tell your good friend Mr. Jeffrey: either he has to let go of all his neuroses, or he will be in a mental institution within ten years—*guaranteed!!!*"

This malediction filled me with a combination of rage and gloom, but I ultimately decided to accept it as a challenge. A few weeks later, after Dorothy had left for a trip to Burma, I dropped by Lalji's and demanded that he qualify what he had said.

He stood by his claim and raised the ante by announcing that as an artist—at the time I was calling myself a sculptor—I was doomed to failure. I was nervous and critical, he declared, and therefore could never produce anything that did not reflect neurosis and criticism.

"I will give you a challenge," he said. "I challenge you to create something—one thing, however small, however large!—that does not reflect the fact that you are both completely dissatisfied and highly critical of everything in the world!"

"But you haven't even seen my work!" I stormed.

Still, when I left Nepal after that first visit, I couldn't help but wonder if he had a point. As long as I can remember, I've always been inclined to see the worst in myself—a masochistic quirk that forced me to accept Lalji's harsh judgment of me while simultaneously proving it to be true.

Over the next few years I found myself continually dredging up Lalji's rude diagnosis, and wondering how much my neuroses actually contribute, for better or worse, to my creative temperament. What would happen if I ever *did* achieve a nonneurotic state? Could I still produce anything worthwhile? I mean, don't all artists create by reproducing their identity in every single work they fashion? And isn't it precisely this quirky sense of self—call it "neurosis" if you will—that gives body to an artist's style, that fleshes out his or her portfolio?

These questions bedeviled me as much as—or more than—the image of myself bouncing off the walls of a padded cell. And so, when I returned to Nepal for the second time in 1983, I felt compelled to seek out Lalji once again. He had identified my particular poison; perhaps he could supply the antidote as well.

His wife met me at the door of their home and directed me toward the yard. Perhaps, over the past four years, I had romanticized my image of Lalji just a bit. At any rate, the figure I saw was hardly the earnest, learned *ascetic* of memory and imagination.

He had clearly put on some weight—but this in itself didn't surprise me, given the time-honored Asian tradition of corpulent gurus. No, what really threw me for a loop was the sight of Lalji in Ray-Bans, lounging on a lawn chair, leafing through a copy of *OMNI* and helping himself from a carton of—Marlboros!

"It can't be!" I cried. "An enlightened soul like yourself, indulging in one of the most repulsive and self-destructive habits in the world! Tell me, dear Lalji: how do you reconcile your spiritual pretensions with the consumption of fine Virginia tobacco?"

"Mr. Jeffrey!"

Lalji folded up his magazine, dropped it onto the grass, and beamed with apparent delight. Without missing a beat, he launched into reciting a parable about a great saint, an ancient guru from South India, whose only mortal shortcoming was a voracious and incorrigible appetite for food.

"This guru would often jump up"—Lalji leaped from his chair—"right in the middle of the most profound discourses, and run wildly into the kitchen to see exactly what was being served, in what quantity, and, most importantly, *when.*

"'Be still!' his wife would chastise him. 'It's your food; no one else will take it! What will people say, seeing you always jumping like this? Here you are, a saddhu, a holy man, preaching temperance but unable to control your appetite!'

"'Dear wife,' the guru replied earnestly, 'do not worry that I must cling to this one thing; it is all that is holding me to the earth! When you see that I have at last lost my appetite for food, only wait; in three days I will be completely gone.'"

The rest of the story, of course, followed faithfully—the guru did indeed lose his appetite, and in short order he had vanished; simply vanished, without a trace.

"An enlightened being on the earth must find an anchor," Lalji said. "Or else he will simply blow away. He is like a man who has climbed to the top of a high, windy peak with an open parachute. The moment he loses his grasp on some earthly thing, he is gone. To take flight from that point—to *actually fly*—is the easiest thing."

I nodded, helped myself to a smoke, and settled back into a chair. I told Lalji that while I didn't entirely agree with his point of view about my art, I was ready to accept some kind of mental exercise that I might use in dealing with my anxieties and neuroses—an Eastern process that might work where my Western techniques had failed. I wanted to learn how to exploit my creative drive—that potent pushy force—without actually having to give up my all-important ego.

"I can give you a solution," Lalji rejoined immediately. "I require only this: do not ask *why* it works. The only important thing is that it works. Long before people knew about carbohydrates and sugars, they were nourished by apples! What if they had refused to eat apples until they could understand exactly why those apples were of any use? So! You don't question why an apple nourishes you. You just eat, and it nourishes! This process I teach you will be the same."

He instructed me to sit back in my straw chair, with my arms out. "Can you feel your heartbeat in your index finger?" I replied that I could. "Look at your fingers," he said. "I want you to imagine, one at a time, flames coming from each finger."

He joined with me in this difficult exercise, at which I was not what you might call successful. Once all our fingers were ostensibly lit, like candles, he began playing with the fire in his hands: waving it, swooping and juggling it. "It is just like this," he said, hands dancing with invisible energies. "You will juggle those flames—the flames that are flowing, wasted, from your fingertips. You will roll them and juggle them. And then—maybe you will feel they are getting a bit heavy, yes? And you will find, you will perceive this heaviness, and when this happens you"—he quickly inverted his hands above his head, eyes closed—"Whoosh! Like this! You let all the energy re-enter you, flow back into you."

He leaned forward, a flash in his eye. "You can even do it in bed—during sex! Even if you are in deep intercourse, you can do this thing and—whoosh!—the woman you are with will also feel it! And the next day she might say, 'You know, I felt something very fine!' Because if you are so intimately connected the energy will circle through both of you— in the form of great ecstasy!

"If you are doing this for a few months, you will begin to change. Maybe your anger will increase a bit, and your sexual energies will go up four or five times what they are now. The anger will pass; it's the only disagreeable part of the cycle. And if you keep this up, I promise you, in one or two years you will be a completely changed person. The flames will cleanse you entirely, burn all the garbage out.

"But listen carefully to what I say now. After six months or a year of concentrated practice, if you go into a dark room and do this, there will be actual visible light—a pale, bluish light—coming from your fingers. And if any friend is with you, he can see this also, all around you. He might say, 'I see some kind of pale, bluish light, but I cannot find its source.' You will be that source!

"This is really the perfect exercise for you, for your special situation." Lalji settled back in his lawn chair, tapped a cigarette from its box. "All your powers are concentrated in your hands. Now they just flow out, useless, and you're waving your hands around and biting your fingers. Do this instead. And keep a flame burning, whenever you can, to guide you. Carry candles with you all the time; make sure you are always affluent in candles!

"And you can burn them at any time, day or night, because being an artist you know that there is no day or night for such people—only cycles of inspiration or barrenness. Life is a single span, a continuum marked by certain periods and creations. Thus, gradually, will you find your inspiration and creativity increasing—and your work will become enlightening instead of neurotic and critical. Then and only then will you meet my challenge! But until that time it is *impossible.* You cannot create something better than you are.

"Why be satisfied with a penny," he asked, holding his thumb and index finger pinched in front of my eyes, "when you can possess the wealth of all diamonds?"

Shortly after that encounter, when I departed the Kingdom of Nepal in the early autumn of 1984, I carried home the conviction that all things were within my grasp. The world could be my pomegranate, if only I could muster up the self-discipline to perform the simple daily exercise Lalji had recommended.

My resolve got off to a redoubtable start, and for my first month or two back in the United States I practiced the finger-flame meditation religiously. Before long, though, the seductive distractions of dinner parties, live jazz, and safe sex left me too bloated, wired, or exhausted to conduct the visualizations more than once or twice a month.

By mid 1987—as I prepared to embark on the voyage that would take me into Tibet, out of Gosainkund, and through Kathmandu's bustling Buddha emporiums—I was burning candles and focusing on my seething inner powers about as often as I was flossing my teeth.

8

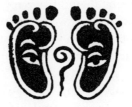

There are many new roads in Kathmandu—the oldest of which is named "New Road."

New Road begins at the Tundhikhel Parade Ground and plows a broad swath through what has become, such as it is, downtown Kathmandu. I steered my rented clunker—an Indian-made Hero bicycle with tassels streaming from the handgrips—through the brightly painted arch, flanked by images of Shiva and Ganesh, and glided to a halt at the first *gundpak* shop on the left. I bought fifteen rupees' worth of the sweet, nutty brown mass. It was wrapped, still warm, in yesterday's New York Stock Exchange report.

Then it was off again, past the shimmering displays of the gem and jewelry shops; past Vision Stationery and New Human Fit Tailors; past shops selling soccer balls and trikes, chutneys and doughnuts, King and Queen commemorative plates and Singer sewing machines; past a crowd of Nepalis massed before a storefront, watching color photographs spew from the maw of an instant processing machine; past the steel-shuttered windows of the American Cultural Center, with their dramatic display of space shuttle photos; past the ancient pipal tree, beneath whose spreading branches lay broad plastic tarps blanketed with rows and rows of local newspapers and magazines; past Central Drug, twenty-one flavors ice cream, Optic Nerve, enormous black bulls chewing complacently in the road as traffic swerved obediently around them—and in the windows of the tour agencies I read the brightly lettered signs saying,

VISIT DAKSHINKALI!
LIVE ANIMAL SACRIFICES
EVERY TUESDAY AND SATURDAY!

At the end of New Road is the old royal palace with its towering pagodas and fantastic courtyards populated by gods, goddesses, and demons. Not a bad venue for some shopping! But before making that plunge into the giddy world of Buddha buying, I cycled around the staid bronze statue of Chandra Shamsher Jung Bahadur Rana, stopped my bicycle, and locked it by a telephone pole at the corner of Dharma Path and New Road. And there I gazed up, face to face with the entrance to the city's most grotesque capitalist monument: three tiers of sooty raw concrete, and a hand-lettered blue and white sign reading "Super Market." This was Bishal Bazaar, Kathmandu's first enclosed shopping mall: a mere seven years old, but already ancient.

I'll tell you why I stopped. Some friends had come to town a couple of weeks earlier, and they returned from a stroll one afternoon to inform me that the management of this so-called Super Market had just finished installing an attraction that had proved to be the modern-day equivalent of the Hanging Gardens of Babylon. We're talking about Kathmandu's very first escalator, linking the first and second floors of the gritty enclosed mall.

Now, I'd been by before, hoping to find this marvel of technology in action. As a rule it was broken, covered over with enormous sheets of plastic, like a minor work by Christo. Today, though, contrary to any of my expectations, the escalator was running; and this I had to see.

There were two enormous crowds. One was gathered at the foot of the escalator, where a sneering guard wielding a nightstick pushed the bravest of the brave, one by one, onto the veranda, the no-man's-land at the base of the procession of hypnotic, endlessly ascending steps. A barefoot porter in filthy, tattered rags—some lost refugee from the hills—stood immobilized at the starting line, awed to paralysis by the stream of metal that flowed as if by divine writ from beneath the rubber cowl by his toes. As I watched, I realized that the man was experiencing a beatific transformation. His knees weakened; and within a moment he was bowing, praying, practically prostrating himself before this divine sight, this river of steel issuing miraculously out of the ground, just as the holy Ganges flows from the scalp of the great Lord Shiva! The guard reached forward and jerked him rudely aside.

The next victim was a twelve-year-old boy who, poised at the bottom, eyed the rise with all the trepidation of a diver who suddenly realizes that, yeah, the high board is really a lot higher than it looks. . . . He swung his arms and heaved a deep breath before closing his eyes and plunging out in his best urban swan dive. Right behind him was an elderly Moslem lady who took one look and tried frantically to back away; instead, she somehow stumbled *onto* the device. At first she kept her eyes closed and seemed to heave a sigh of relief as her senses convinced her that she wasn't moving after all. But as soon as she opened them, her face whitened into a mask of absolute and abject horror. She clung desperately to the rubber rail, crouched as if for combat as her sisters, her husband, her sons and grandsons all faded, perhaps forever, against the backdrop of blinking advertisements far below.

The second mob waited at the escalator's summit, delighting in the huge joke of relative motion. These sophisticated voyeurs—many of them seasoned escalator veterans themselves—shouted with glee as each of the hapless riders was propelled, panicked and staggering, from the apparently motionless safety of the escalator onto the utterly unexpected menace presented by stable ground.

I ran up and down the stairway parallel to the marvelous escalator, enslaved by the realization that I could not leave, could not bear to leave, before demonstrating my utter command, my consummate prowess with escalators. No; I positively could not continue my search for a perfect peaceful Buddha before leaping onto this escalator like a trapeze artist, and wowing these local yokels with a bit of spontaneous street theater.

So, after mingling patiently with the downstairs mob (who ushered me forward with the respect and generosity characteristic of all Nepalis), I found myself at the coveted brink. At first I made a show of trying to back away—and then, letting loose an awful howl, mounted the flying stairway in the most histrionic fashion imaginable, a pantomime of sheer terror, flailing and doubling back, slipping down the railing, disappearing from sight, finally rising to my feet only to be propelled like a rag doll into the waiting arms of the electrified crowd.

Ah, they roared! They loved it! These people! *My* people! I walked back down the steps, Nepalis slapping me on the back. Whew! Hey! What a riot! That was great! *I* was great!

But then the grin slid off my face like a wet towel, because the crowd was captured by a momentary silence. Far below, making their way through the swinging glass doors, a retinue of Buddhist monks entered the Shopping Center. They approached in single file, heads shaven, their robes flowing behind them like a flood of freshly squeezed Florida orange juice.

61

The crowd melted, parting like a biblical sea to allow them through. The guard abashedly lowered his nightstick and stepped hastily aside. And the monks, without panic or ceremony, simply mounted the escalator and

    rode it

      to the next

        level.

9

Mornings, everywhere in the world, take their own peculiar rhythms; carefully etched compromises between the body's perpetual reluctance and civilization's unflagging persistence. My experience in Kathmandu was no exception.

Wake up for the first time at 5:15 in the morning to the crunch of army boots on loose gravel, and hoarse crowing. The troops from the Police Training Academy just down the block have begun their morning march, rousing the neighborhood roosters. Cram head between pillows; fall back to sleep.

Wake up for the second time at precisely 6:30 A.M. to the ceaseless, strident ringing of a *puja* bell, accompanied by guttural chants: an anonymous neighbor is conducting his morning ritual. By now the sky is lightening. Within another thirty minutes the morning commute has begun, roaring and honking around the blind corner some twenty feet from my bedroom window. No more sleeping after this.

Consciousness is inevitably followed by a trumpeting of the bowels. Run to the bathroom and expel the previous day's consortium of microscopic invaders. Shower, keeping my mouth clamped shut to prevent ingesting even a drop of the deadly local water (I actually knew one woman who showered with a snorkel).

These ablutions complete, I throw on my robe and flip-flops and wander outside to check for the daily delivery of the *Rising Nepal,* the country's lightweight English-language daily. I carry the newspaper into the dining room, settle myself in a lopsided cane chair, and spread the tabloid open on the table, eager to digest the latest news and opinion of my favorite Hindu kingdom.

Fainting Spells in School

The girl students currently enrolled at the proposed school at Kakarvitta are having fainting spells all of a sudden, it is learnt.

Fifteen students suddenly fainted last Sunday for about forty-five minutes.

It is claimed that the phenomenon began after the school felled a tree which was long regarded as the abode of Bandevi to make way for the construction of an annexe.

A puja was organised last Sunday to appease the goddess but fifteen girl students again fainted right there, sources close to the school said.

However, the girls have not been medically examined.

10th Day on Bridge

The wounded black cow on Bagmati Bridge has entered her tenth day on the sidewalk, while authorities have yet to show that they have noticed her plight.

The animal looks much weaker, and cannot even lift her head to take a sip from an earthen bowl of water left there by some kindly soul.

Passing pedestrians have reacted with compassion leaving maize leaves for the cow to eat while an ascetic from a nearby ghat has covered her in straw to protect the animal from the hot sun and rains.

A glaring need for a better management of the city's urban livestock is called for. And this is reflected in the sad story of the cow on the bridge. Her plight seems to be no one's concern in the world's only Hindu Kingdom.

Doctors Dismissed

Four doctors dismissed from the Department of Health Services. Dr. Chetri, Dr. Agarwal, Dr. Sharma and Dr. Amatya have been relieved of their posts. These doctors did not report to duty for the past five to seven years.

I skim through a riot of other compelling headlines: "FARMER DIES OF IGNORANCE"—"SURVEY TO ASCERTAIN EXACT LOCATION OF NEPAL"—"INDIAN PLANE FAILS TO LAND"—"MAJORITY OF SHOPKEEPERS STOP THROWING GARBAGE"—ultimately arriving at the Letters page.

Dear Editor:

This refers to the news item on scientist Shaha. The *Rising Nepal,* 25 August issue states that Mr. Shaha is the inventor of a plant that "generates energy through gravitation, without using any kind of fuel."

His Majesty's Government, which "provided him with financial as well as other assistance to invent the fuel-saving plant" can duly claim a major part of the acclaim and glory that follows such an epoch-making venture. In this critical hour of mankind's history when the human race is faced with an energy famine and an eventual heat-death of the universe under the inexorable Second Law of Thermodynamics, no stone must be left unturned to bootleg on energy supplies.

I had the good fortune to listen to Mr. Shaha explaining his device to a skeptical but apathetic group of engineers at the Pulchowk Campus. His device basically consists of a big equilateral triangle with heavy metallic spheres at the vertices and smaller equilateral triangle with smaller spheres revolving around an axis. According to the inventor, the force of gravitational attraction between the spheres will propel the smaller sphere toward the larger one—first one, then the other, then the third in a perpetual dance of cosmic eternity. A generator fixed to the revolving axis would then provide free electricity.

The National Council for Science and Technology, the highest authority in the land on matters so abstruse, provided about 70,000 rupees to effect this historic invention. I would like to thank our learned doctors in the Council for providing every Nepali the opportunity to be a co-partner in this great venture of harnessing perpetual motion. . . .

At exactly 8 A.M., Krishna, cook and housekeeper *sans* rival, Master of Baked Goods and Doctor of Lasagna, rides his bicycle in through the gate and parks it on the cement drive. Krishna is a tiny man (even petite women dwarf him), in his late fifties or early sixties, with sparse hair and a perpetual hound-dog expression. One gets the feeling that a strong cat could knock him down just by rubbing against his legs. His diminutive appearance, however, belies an awesome expertise. In a country where expatriate Westerners, for lack of other substantial grievances, argue long and loud about the relative skill and inventiveness of their cooks, Krishna was the last word. His gifts in the kitchen are legendary.

We greet each other with a warm *namasté*—the beautiful local salutation that means "I greet the God that dwells within you"—and I write a letter or two while he prepares breakfast: a mug of strong Indian coffee, a bowl of sliced mangoes and tangerine with yogurt, and banana pancakes topped with maple syrup and butter. Eggs and egg dishes are to be avoided at all cost in Kathmandu, where the chickens are fattened on fish meal and a horrible, fishy essence thus pervades everything from omelettes to french toast.

To live in Kathmandu, including half the rent on a very comfortable little house (which I shared with a wonderfully convivial but usually absent Asiaphile, teacher, trek leader, and caroms champ named Ray Rodney); the salary for Raj, our gardener; the *dhoti*, who arrived every Wednesday and Sunday to haul our laundry down to the river for a good beating; and 1,500 rupees a month for Krishna, who made the best carrot cake, pumpkin pie, coleslaw, and baked turkey I have ever tasted; all this, including groceries, came to about $175 dollars a month.

I studied Krishna with unending fascination. In a country full of mysteries, he was the ultimate enigma. And the more I watched him go about his business, the more I thought of Hesse's *Journey to the East*. In that saga it was Leo, the expedition's servant, who turned out to be the enlightened being they would learn their lessons from. Krishna was justly famous as one of the best cooks in town—he could prepare everything from Dutch apple pie to egg rolls; from Indian curries to the meanest *dhalbhat* (the traditional Nepali meal of lentil stew over rice) in the Valley. He would work all day, with never a complaint or sour expression, and then sit in the kitchen on a rattan stool doing *absolutely nothing* as Ray and I ate our dinner, played music, and had loud, raucous fêtes with our expat' chums. When we were quite finished, Krishna slid into the dining room (as noiselessly as the proud Snake Gods who once inhabited the valley) and cleaned up after us, silent and expressionless but without a trace of resentment.

After completing his work, Krishna would get onto his bicycle and return home; home being a five-story tall building with a panoramic view of the Himalayas, located just off New Road—one of the most expensive districts in town. But Krishna is not a tenant; he *owns* the building. He and his family occupy the top two stories, and he rents out the lower three. In his other, parallel life, our humble cook and servant is the patriarch of a large and well-respected clan, which includes two enormous sons, both of whom are world-class soccer players thrice their father's size.

And here in this well-groomed nest in the center of downtown, the roles are reversed, and it is Krishna who is the benevolent despot; for that is the way in Hindu households.

Through the length of my stay in Kathmandu, I was moved to regard our domestic help with a mixture of awe, respect, and pure bewilderment. I kept trying, and failing, to imagine a similar situation in the West: a moneyed landlord and head of household working overtime as a manservant, at the beck and call of wild and crazy foreigners.

After finishing my breakfast, the rest of my ritual was simple: brush up the teeth with boiled and filtered water, make a few calls, take care of any sundry business that I was not able to put off another day, present Krishna with the current dinner fantasy, and outfit myself for an afternoon of cycling from shop to shop beneath the grab-bag cloud cover of Kathmandu Valley.

But first, more important than any weather report, was the daily status check on the crow. The crow! Two weeks before, as Ray and I were emptying our dinner plates in preparation for a dessert of Krishna's homemade brownies topped with Mango Tango ice cream from Nirula's Hot Shoppe, we saw the sky light up with a fantastic blue flash and heard a tremendous explosion. (Holy fuck: they've bombed the palace!) We ran to the door—saw nothing—no indication that any civil disaster, on any scale, had occurred.

The following morning, Ray—who is unusually sensitive to the subtle signs, symbols, and metaphors offered by our environment—beckoned me outside. He did not look pleased. In fact, he wore the baleful look of a man who has just received a very unpleasant telegram. He pointed up-ward—I followed his gaze and winced, remembering last night's deafening blast.

A huge black crow had lighted on the electrical wires outside our house, and his touchdown had somehow caused a short circuit. The bird, upside down and fried to a crisp, now hung by its talons, permanently welded to the line about twenty feet above our front gate.

Over the next few days, mutual friends gleefully pointed out, to Ray and myself, that nothing is permanent. The crow could not dangle in the air forever. Someday, in the not-too-distant future—tomorrow, maybe—its legs would rot out and the abomination would fall to earth, exploding onto the street in an infested mass too horrible to imagine. One would not want to be below the wire, occupying that particular square yard of real estate, when this happened; the experience could put a severe damper on a day of spiritual materialism. Every day, therefore, I carefully took note of the luckless fowl's position and fed myself a subliminal reminder to give the area under the power lines plenty of berth.

Today it looked good—if "good" is the proper word to describe a decaying crow. Both claws appeared firmly fastened to the wire. Little likelihood, unless a strong wind came up, that the inauspicious delicacy would choose today for its final descent. I heaved a sigh of relief, slung my daypack over my shoulder—in Kathmandu, day and night, all *sahibs* and *memsahibs* are committed marsupials—and launched myself into the wonderful world of Buddha-shopping.

10

It may seem strange, this whole idea of shopping for gods and goddesses and Buddhas—but just looking at the kinds of products for sale in the shops and cold stores, one comes to realize that devotion and commercialism have long gone hand-in-hand in Nepal: Buddha Fruits, Lord Ganesh potato chips, Tara mayonnaise. There's an openness, a streetcorner accessibility, a *vulgarity* to the gods and goddesses of Nepal that you just don't see in the West. No Yahweh toothpaste here, or Baby Jesus Electrical Works; no Moses cigarettes, or Mary Magdelene communion wafers. Our gods and prophets don't endorse soft drinks or sell potato chips. We take them seriously. And you take them seriously, too, or we'll hang you by your elbows. . . .

Asia is a mythical jubilee, full of characters more lively and entertaining than anything you'll find at Disneyland. Especially Nepal, Land of 10,000 Gods, where even everyday worship is laced with an alchemical magic. Shiva and Shakti blink on and off in Christmas lights; Vishnu gestures benevolently from the cover of a comic book; gilded cobra gods rise, hoods flared and tongues flickering, atop pedestals in public pools.

No, they are not as anal with their gods as we Westerners are—which is one reason why they were easier to steal than one might think. The only outsiders who really took the Hindu gods absolutely seriously were the Moslems, who smashed idols and set temples ablaze during their antipagan romps through northern India in the eleventh through fourteenth centuries. That was a big mistake. If those Islamic marauders had been more clever, they would have simply carted the best work back home in carefully padded crates and recited the Koran in the empty vestibules as the treasures slowly but surely appreciated in value. Which is, of course, precisely what the Chinese did in Tibet, minus the Koran-chanting business.

None of this is meant to imply that the Nepalis treat their devotional statues lightly. True, some are made for the sole purpose of being hawked to souvenir hunters. But before a given idol or sculpture is considered fit for devotion, it must first undergo an ancient rite called *Kumbhubhishekham*. During this complex ceremony, the spirit of the god or goddess is coaxed down to the earth and persuaded to leave just a tiny bit of divine essence within the previously inanimate stone.

Besides the various on-sale deities, the main players in this shopping game were the shopkeepers themselves—a highly savvy bunch, usually honest, sometimes cunning, but always finely tuned to the machinations of the Western mind.

One of the more attractive things about Asian art is that it doesn't glorify individual artists the way the Western world does. Bidders at an auction in Los Angeles, to pick one particularly perverse example, recently spent thousands upon thousand of dollars for cardboard boxes full of anonymous office trash, simply because Andy Warhol was the one who went around and emptied the wastebaskets.

In Asia, even the most exquisite Buddhas and Taras are traditionally unsigned, reflecting the belief that the human artist is merely a tool, a channel for the genius of Vishwakarma, the divine architect.

During my first visits to Nepal, hailing directly from a country where important artists are ranked just a notch below rock and roll stars, I felt a definite impatience with the staid traditionalism of Eastern devotional art. Why couldn't it break through its boundaries and become . . . *more?* All it needed, I reckoned, was a sentient boot in the ass from some innovative maverick artist; something to kick it into the twentieth century, or at least integrate it with modern (that is, Western) styles of expression.

Looking for the shoe that might deliver such a kick, I made it a point to visit exhibitions of contemporary Nepalese art wherever and whenever possible. I was in search of that elusive quantity: an Eastern Picasso—or at least a Giotto— who could breathe new life into the tired old forms. What I found surprised me. The whole clogged flue of Western art history, from cubism to fauvism and up through the chimney of abstract expressionism, was represented. One amazing thing about developing nations: when anything happens, from traffic to modern art, it happens all at once. Fauvism; surrealism; minimalism; all, like amateur climbers on a nasty cliff, were floundering for toeholds. The results of these efforts were sometimes inveigling, but usually imitative and embarrassing.

I did come across a number of interesting and original paintings, by artists such as B. G. Baidya, Manuj Babu Mishra, Paramesh Adhikari, and Ragini Upadhyay; bright or brutal canvases that seemed to be making a point, and might have shown well in the more fearless corners of lower Manhattan or L.A. By and large, though, the situation looked grim. There was some tentative flirting, but nobody had a stiff enough broom to sweep Central Asia off its feet.

I found this fact inexplicably frustrating. One problem, I reasoned, might be that almost all of Nepal's contemporary artists had received Western-style training. It seemed unlikely that truly original ideas could spring from such a contrived background. Maybe that fateful kick would have to come from someone who had been schooled in the most traditional of arts.

Following that thread I wandered through the alleyways of Thamel and Taleju, dropping in on studios and talking to the best traditional artists I could find. These were all young lamas who paint exquisite devotional canvases known, in the Tibetan tradition, as *thangkas*. All these artists had studied, from an early age, under traditional masters; all now earned their keep by producing a stream of work that was utterly derivative. Often enough, their paintings were copied directly from books or other thangkas. It seemed a horrible waste. All the artists were impressively talented. A few were nothing less than inspired and created breathtakingly detailed work using natural stone colors, the grinding and mixing of which is an art in itself.

Didn't it drive them crazy? Weren't they totally frustrated? Didn't they feel an overpowering urge to break from the fold and establish their identities as original, individual names on the Asian art scene? I asked these questions over and over again. The answers were often confused and occasionally eloquent, but they were always no. It was mind-bending; but by the time I left the kingdom, my understanding of Eastern art had undergone a radical change.

If Nepali artists are not overcome by a zeal to produce contemporary work, it is not by virtue of incompetence. Beautiful paintings, sculptures, and ceramics abound, but every single work has a specific—and ancient—devotional purpose. Sometimes the works are beautiful because of their purpose—like the brilliantly colored prayer flags that festoon high hillsides and monasteries. Sometimes the art is beautiful *in spite of* its purpose—like the sumptuous idols at Dakshinkali, scarlet with the blood of sacrificed goats.

The most perfect art, according to the Nepalis, stems from the re-creation of perfected formulas. No attempt need be made to realign (much less to shatter) the age-old symbolic infrastructure. Why? Because it isn't necessary. If you can comprehend the symbol at its deepest, most primal level, the image—of a Buddha or Krishna or Tara—can hike your valence just as effectively as a work by Joseph Beuys, Sue Coe, or Clemente.

It's the difference between "yogic" and "athletic" art. Artists in the Western world work by bending the banister, confident that anyone sitting on it will slide into a new awareness. Our art, objective and nonobjective alike, flexes its muscles and pushes. It's no surprise that contemporary artists have, through the ages, encountered resistance and even scorn; theirs is the burden of dragging the public, kicking and screaming, toward a new awareness of form and self. The art object in the West is not a final destination; it is a place marker in uncharted territory, a piton hammered into the face of a mountain of indeterminate height.

In Nepal, traditional art is believed to already contain the highest level of understanding possible. Thangkas and dances, bronze Buddhas and ritual bells, all take their shapes from tested formulas, tried and true guidelines firmly anchored in enlightenment.

The sole responsibility of the artist is to express these formulas as faithfully as possible. There is no need to shock the audience, seduce powerful gallery owners, or grope after an individual style. The whole idea of an ego is, after all, a bit beside the point—the one being recognized is God.

Given this information it's not difficult to see why Nancy and I—embarked on another casual afternoon of spiritual materialism—were thrown for a loop when one Mr. S. R. Aryal, proprietor of the Deity Depot on Dorbar Marg, emphatically introduced us to the work of a specific human being: an elderly sculptor from the neighboring city of Patan named Sidhi Raj.

Aryal's art collection was the most dense and fascinating I'd seen. Much of it was in the setting; the shop interior was dark and mysterious, slightly musty, lush with art. A potted ivy sat by the door; its tendrils crept up the frame and spread across the ceiling, twisting between the spotlights and piquing my unspoken fear that Kathmandu was becoming, at least for me, a kind of Buddha-buying jungle. Patches of stray light filtered in through the window, glinting off the naked arms, legs, and thrice-bent torsos of bronze gods and goddesses that crammed every available inch of shelf space. Tibetan saddle carpets and prayer blankets were piled high against one wall; the showcases were filled to capacity with amulet boxes, ritual daggers, bowls containing silver beads, amber, and turquoise.

Everything in the shop had integrity. There was no junk; Aryal's eye for statues was eclectic and tasteful. He himself was short and stout, with serious eyes, a pocked complexion, and a sparse mustache dusted onto his upper lip. Something about his personality exuded a quiet wisdom that neither Nancy nor I felt qualified to ignore. We felt compelled to trust Aryal's judgment—and his judgment was that Sidhi Raj was the first and last word in serious Buddha investing.

It was Sidhi Raj, Aryal told us, whose statues were continually sought after by dealers, curators, and lamas. It was Sidhi Raj who was keeping the high art of Nepali bronze casting alive. And—more to the point—it was the work of Sidhi Raj that would appreciate most swiftly in value.

As if to prove this point, Aryal raised his prices every time we dropped in. . . .

The salesman's enthusiasm and conviction were so palpable, such an effective sales technique, that after only a few more visits to the Deity Depot, Nancy and I were caught in the grip of an invincible obsession. The first question we'd ask on walking into any shop became "Do you have anything by Sidhi Raj?" We determined that there must have been more and more buyers privy to this "inside information"—practically overnight, every half-pint gallery in town claimed to be representing the Raj clan.

But in short order we began to observe, to our confusion and chagrin, that much of this abundant new work peddled off under the "Raj" name was amateurish in the worst way.

Why? We put the question to Aryal, who offered what seemed to be a reasonable explanation. Even though Sidhi Raj himself might have indeed sculpted the original plaster models from which the molds for these statues were taken, an equal amount of talent is needed to whip the nascent casting into shape. Those castings emerge from the mold looking raw as radishes; it takes a carver of great skill to bring out the highlights, the exquisite little details, intended by the artist.

With the tourist community clamoring for topnotch devotional art, Aryal explained, old Sidhi's homegrown foundry had begun to churn statues out one after the other, handing the unfinished bronzes over to his ragged little nephews for the cleaning, carving, and finishing touches.

Henry Ford might have been impressed; but as far as Nancy and I were concerned, this mass production represented a dangerous trend indeed.

As the days went by, the quest for a quality work by Sidhi Raj began to seem all but futile. The market was flooded with work, some of it good, much of it junk; and everybody was calling everything a Raj.

One afternoon, as I sat at home devouring a pumpkin pie and slaving over an incendiary letter about taxi horns to the *Rising Nepal*, I heard a frantic knock upon my door. It was Nancy, flushed and breathless. Her eyes were wild.

"You've got to come down to the Deity Depot with me," she gasped. "Aryal just showed me a fantastic little Buddha, and I don't know what to do."

I raced into the garage to get my bicycle and found Krishna sitting with Raj, the household's young gardener. They were at their ease, listening to Radio Nepal and smoking Laligurans filters. Rising nobly at my request, they pumped air into the vehicle's beleaguered tires and sent me on my way.

We flew along the dusty, gravel-strewn roads. Past a bunch of boys playing Ping-Pong on a makeshift table, using a row of bricks as their net. . . .

. . . Past Elsie the cow, who burst out of a thick copse of *ganja* shrubs as we rode past, her head rearing and eyes rolling. . . .

. . . Past a toothless woman strolling down the road, holding the leash of a black goat in one hand and a carved walking stick in the other . . .

. . . and around the gold cobra capital rising from the murky pool of Nag Pokhari: Snake Lake.

Down the hill. Now we were really in town. We cycled past the cinema, its parking lot crowded with snack stalls;

past the brightly painted shingle announcing "LALJI: HAND ANALYST"; past the elephant cage fence that defines the Royal Palace. We were just about to turn onto Durbar Marg—the broad avenue that begins at the Palace Gate—when we were forced to a halt.

"Stop!" A Nepali policeman accosted us, overflowing with an urgent sense of mission. "You must wait! The King is coming!"

There was no doubt about it. A huge crowd thronged the sidewalks all the way down broad Durbar Marg. Policemen with woven cane riot shields stood guard every three or four meters, some chatting self-consciously into loaf-sized walkie-talkies.

A palpable enthusiasm hung in the air. The Nepalis shifted around us like agitated molecules, speaking in short, enthusiastic bursts. The woman we had seen leading the goat caught up to us; she forced her walking stick into a little patch of earth and tethered the animal to it. Three old men squatted by the entrance to the Gaida Wildlife Camp office entrance, their baggy drawstring pants billowing onto the ground as they passed a smouldering clay *chilum* among themselves. Little girls perched on their fathers' shoulders, clutching red paper flags.

Neither bicycles nor cars are permitted to park on an avenue that will be graced by the supreme presence of the King of Nepal—a man who is touted as a modern incarnation of Vishnu, the Great Preserver. Windows are shuttered and curtains drawn, giving the normally frenetic boulevard an austere, model railroad town appearance. As Nancy and I walked our bikes along the sidewalk, we came across a poignant sight. Some poor ignoramus, uninformed of the pending procession, had left his car parked unattended on Durbar Marg. A Nepali tow truck—a crane, essentially—was loading it onto a flatbed truck as a mass of spectators watched in awe. The Toyota sedan dangled in the air, twisting slowly in the breeze. Nancy and I watched the loading process until it was over, and the flatbed roared away and disappeared around the corner in a cloud of black diesel smoke.

Nancy turned to the man beside her, who had just bent over to light up a cigarette.

"Where will they take that car?" she asked.

He cast her a baleful eye. "To a lonely place," he replied.

After what seemed like an eternity, an eerie hush descended like a fog bank on the masses. A tiny crackling sound, like frying guppies, could be heard in the distance: applause for the royal motorcade as it emerged from the palace parking lot around the corner. The oddly restrained clapping—more appropriate for a retirement dinner than the appearance of Lord Vishnu's human incarnation—dominoed down the sidewalk, finally engulfing us. We craned forward as the vehicles blinked by.

The King of Nepal, Sri Panch Maharaja Birendra Bir Bikram Shah Dev, waved cheerfully to his constituents from behind the wheel of a vintage Corvette. He was alone in the car, but surrounded on all sides by military police on motorcycles. His informal attire suggested he might be going to a wedding; he wore a sports jacket, white tunic, and colorful *topi*—the soft, fez-shaped hat that serves Nepali protocol much like the Western tie.

Sri, incidentally, is a term of lofty respect in Nepal and India, equivalent to "lord" or "saint." And *panch* means "five." The royal epithet, "Sri Panch," is simply a shortcut for saying "Sri Sri Sri Sri Sri"—"saint" to the fifth power.

I craned my neck for a look at the Corvette's rear bumper, imagining how refreshing it would be to see some hint at humor, any indication of a personality behind the royal mask, expressed with a cunning bumper sticker like "Don't Follow Me, I'm Lost," or "My Other Vehicle Is Garuda."

"Yes, As a Matter of Fact, I Do Own the Whole Goddamn Road!"

"Kings Give a Royal Fuck."

"Shit Happens."

Needless to say, there was nothing on the bumper but brightly polished chrome.

As the procession zipped out of sight, I was struck by an unnerving coincidence: His Royal Highness bore an uncanny resemblance to my cousin Richie, a certified public accountant living in Deer Park, Long Island.

The strangely un-Nepali silence returned for a split second; then it disintegrated. Traffic flooded the street, horns blasted, and Durbar Marg regressed to its natural state of pandemonium.

There were a couple of collectors at the Depot when we arrived. Nancy looked around in a panic and heaved an audible sigh of relief when she spied the little *repoussé* Buddha still meditating contentedly on its shelf. The moment the other customers—our sworn rivals—left, she glanced at Aryal. He nodded, removed the statue from its place, and brought it over to show us.

It was tiny, but absolutely exquisite, with a little ruby set into its urna. And the piece, Aryal assured us with a twinkle in his eye, was by the hand of Sidhi Raj himself. It had to be, he explained, because this was not a cast piece at all. It had been executed in repoussé: a technique that involves painstakingly hammering a sheet of copper into a finely sculpted mold. Considered the hallmark of an expert metalsmith, repoussé is a one-person job; no twelve-year-olds need apply. And, of course, this astral level of expertise was reflected by the statue's truly lavish price tag.

The first time Nancy had seen this piece, she had scrutinized it for nearly an hour, making every attempt to weigh its attributes against its flaws. Most of the "flaws," I soon discovered, were unavoidable; they were a function of the process of repoussé itself. On closer inspection, though, they did seem a bit iffy; the hand had a rather paddlelike look, for sure, and there was a clumsy, scarlike seam showing down the back. There was also, needless to say, the size factor. If the statue had been any smaller, you could have worn it around your neck.

And so I found myself, once again, undertaking a process at which I was quickly becoming an expert: searching for points of irritation in an image of the Buddha.

Nancy and I argued the issue back and forth, rocking from one position to the other like elephants caught in a mire. Finally we reached a total impasse. The statue was great, it had its problems, the detail was fabulous, the seam was showing, the expression was celestial, the price was astronomical, and hey! How did we even know that it *was* by Sidhi Raj?

Aryal must have been anticipating this very thought. He picked up the statue, turned it upside down, and squinted at the bottom as if noticing it for the first time. Then he beckoned us forward.

"Look."

He pointed toward the edge of the oval of copper that sealed the statue's base. Were my eyes deceiving me? No; there it was, eminently readable and rendered in the unmistakable flowing script of the Nepali language. One word, etched awkwardly into the metal:

"SIDHI."

The Buddha was signed!

"Incredible," I said. "I never thought I'd live to see the day. What say, Nance?

"Nance?"

But she was in a trance—signing away her travelers' checks like lightning.

11

Now that Nancy had her heart's desire, there was no particular reason for her to hang around in dusty, noisy Kathmandu. She and Rick, deciding they needed a little vacation, set off post-haste for Royal Chitwan National Park—a steamy jungle preserve full of leopard, deer, and rhinoceros, deep in the Terai Desert of southern Nepal—

—leaving me with a wad o' cash, and no likely prospects in sight. I shopped alone, accompanied only by a mounting sense of pressure. Prices continued to soar. Meanwhile, dozens of Japanese dealers combed the streets of Kathmandu, sometimes buying out entire galleries in one fell swoop.

There was a place right down the block from Hanuman Dhoka—the old Palace Square—across the street from what had once, in days of yore, been Kathmandu's only one-hour color lab. My eyes wandered over the neatly ordered row of statues in the window. Hmm. . . .

The interior of the shop was filled with glass cabinets, their insides painted sea green. A long-handled feather duster leaned against the wall. The *sowji* himself was fast asleep, lounging on a pile of cushions behind a display case full of earrings. A massive gold wristwatch hung loosely on his dangling wrist, like a bracelet. An uncanny sixth sense awakened him just as I was about to sneak back out the door. He swung into sitting position, cleared his throat with a horrible, retching gurgle, turned slightly to his left and spat expertly out the door. He then unfolded a pair of horn-rimmed glasses, fixed them on his nose, and faced me with a severe, scholarly eye.

"You are looking for something?"

"Yes. . . ."

He nodded his head earnestly as I described, in a well-practiced soliloquy, precisely what I wanted.

"Well, I have a good Manjushri. . . ."

"Is it by Sidhi Raj?"

He made a sort of churning sound, like water bubbling around inside a camel's hump. "Not Sidhi Raj. Family of Sidhi Raj. Brother of Sidhi Raj. Very good piece."

The shopkeeper opened a glass showcase and removed the Manjushri. I took it in my hands and examined it, not at all displeased. It was wonderful; elegant; perfect. Except for one little thing: the face of Manjushri, from the neck up, was not plain polished metal, but had been beautifully painted in gold, blue, red, and black. Now, this was not unusual; I was looking at the traditional Tibetan style, and it definitely has its appeal. Some people even seem to prefer it; Tibetans, for example. It's also a favorite of the upper-class Japanese, with their taste for Kabuki actors, geisha girls, and heavy makeup in general.

But for me, unh unh. No way. Permanence is of the essence. When I looked at that painstaking paint job, all I could think was, uh oh, that stuff'll start to smear before I even get through LAX customs; it'll wear down and rub off noticeably in a couple of months, getting sloppier and sloppier, until finally, five or ten thousand years from now, when they finally dig this sculpture up from the deep rubble of what was once a fashionable Berkeley neighborhood and set it on a shelf in some post-apocalypse museum, all that will be left of that meticulous face will be a few faded stains, and a little tag attached to Manjushri's arm saying, "Bronze with traces of polychrome." What's the point?

I asked the shop owner if the paint could be removed, but even before he answered I recognized the subtle irony in my request. Even though Manjushri is the god of incisive wisdom, there was really no way to *know*, for certain, what he really looked like. What kind of face was hidden underneath all that paint? I mean, it could be really hideous, the paint could be disguising some terrible flaw in the artistry, and how would I ever have the gall to say, after they'd spent hours scrubbing off that beautifully painted face, "No, thanks, I don't like the curve of the nose . . . sorry, the chin's too weak . . . my mistake, the eyebrows are too Neanderthal. . . ."

So I told him to skip it. He nodded and, undaunted, leaned slightly toward me and asked if I might like to look at some fine new Taras he had just received. They were, he added knowingly, in the *back room*.

Now, Taras are another thing altogether. Let me tell you a bit about the two Taras:

Thirteen hundred years ago, Tsrong-Tsong Gompa—the powerful king of the area now called Tibet—fell into a dilemma rather typical of his times. He had succeeded, through force and intrigue, in securing for himself the entire high plateau between the Chinese empire and the vast Himalayan chain that formed the ambiguous northern border of Nepal. He was king of the hill for the moment; but alliances changed fast in those days.

Not wishing to be swallowed up by the larger fish around him, Tsrong-Tsong Gompa devised a strategic tribute. He demanded one princess from each of the two neighboring realms, to serve as his wives. Having such "hostage" brides from Nepal and China in his court wouldn't permanently forestall hostilities; but they were unlikely to be a concern during his own lifetime.

Tsrong-Tsong Gompa was clever; the Nepalis and Chinese even more so. Well aware of the persuasive powers of their women, each ruler sent over a princess of extraordinary beauty. Both were thoroughly schooled in the sexual secrets of Tantra, as well as in the more esoteric delights of Buddhism. Between the two of them, the mighty Tsrong-Tsong Gompa was converted to Buddhism in very short order—and the Taras were justly rewarded by being reincarnated as bodhisattvas of compassion.

The princess from the verdant Kathmandu Valley came to be known as the "green" Tara. Her colleague from the north was the "white." Both are available at your various art galleries, curio shops, and handicraft concerns all over Kathmandu and Patan. The one difference is that while the White Tara is usually portrayed sitting with her legs crossed, the Green Tara has her right foot resting on a lotus. Needless to say, the Green Tara—Nepal's very own—was the lady I was partial to.

The shopkeeper went from cabinet to cabinet, fetching every one of his Taras. We looked them over, one and all, in search of the four most important attributes: delicate feet; elegantly sculpted hands; gentle, serene smile; and spiritual radiance. And after reviewing every one of these Taras, I was astonished to find that not a single one of them possessed all the qualities I sought in perfect, unassailable proportions.

This one had lovely and expressive hands, but there was something tight and mean about the shape of her lips. . . .

This one had full, softly smiling lips, and crossed eyes. . . .

This one had warm, beguiling eyes but a squat, fat neck. . . .

This one had a svelte, elegant neck and delicious, pouting lips, but no sense of humor. . . .

This one had a great sense of humor, but she didn't seem like the *creative* type. . . .

This one was pretty, funny, and creative, but she wasn't Jewish. . . .

And I wonder why I'm still not married!

12

"Nah nah! You don't know!" Benjamin retorted. "That
Roof of the World makes men like animals! The search for
sacred things makes devils of them! Did people flay and
burn us Jews for the love of money? Nah nah nah! They
did it for religion—for the things they thought are holy!"
—TALBOT MUNDY, *The Devil's Guard*

For six-hundred years, an androgynous statue of Laksmi-Na-
rayan—the left side goddess, the right side god—served as
an oracle for the women of the Kathmandu Valley. According
to legend, the black granite figure had been presented to the
king of Bhaktapur by a *naga*—a Snake King—in return for
having saved the royal serpent's life. Ever since, Bhaktapur's
expectant mothers have traditionally visited the image and
poured oil over its forehead. If the oil flowed down over the
breast of the goddess Laksmi, the baby would likely be a
girl; if it trickled down the chest of Narayan, a boy.

This meter-high statue was one of the most beloved pil-
grimage sites in the Valley, revered for centuries. In February
1984, it was crudely hacked from its shrine and smuggled
from the Kingdom of Nepal.

"Today," the *Rising Nepal* bitterly speculated, "Laksmi-
Narayan probably adorns the spiritually sterile living room
of a Western connoisseur of 'art.'"

Anybody who has spent some time living in Nepal eventually stumbles across at least one of its dark secrets and picks up an axe to grind. For some people, the cause of choice is Nepal's mushrooming drug problem—there are almost 50 times as many heroin addicts in Kathmandu as there were twelve years ago. For others, the bone is government corruption, in and out of the Royal Palace; for still others, it's the Jekyll-and-Hyde face of international aid, which gives the illusion of building up Nepal while often crippling the kingdom's chances for self-sufficiency.

On a strictly personal level, the cultural plunder of Nepal's devotional art has always gotten my blood up. Hoping to expose a few of the kingpins involved in the art trafficking, I sent out a few queries to magazines—and finally got a bite.

My plan was simple: return to Nepal from Tibet in late September and begin making the contacts that would get me in good with the smugglers themselves. It ought to be fairly easy; I had been to Nepal enough times to know the ropes and knew a few people who could probably put me on the right track.

The day after Rick, Nancy, and I had arrived in Tibet—saddle sore and disoriented after the grueling, four-day journey overland from Kathmandu in a cramped, stuffy Toyota Land Cruiser—I found myself relaxing over early morning yak-burgers in the coffee shop of the Lhasa Hotel. My two traveling companions were still in bed, but I was sharing a table with half a dozen other people. A few of them were good friends from Nepal who were working on various long-term projects in Tibet. There were also a number of other expat's I'd never met.

"So what brings you to Asia this time?" someone asked.

"Oh, not much. Just seein' the sights. . . ." Giddy from the altitude—we had gained nearly ten thousand feet in four days—I started babbling recklessly about my novel, a few ideas, and the art-smuggling story. "You know I think it's one of the more disgusting scams going down around here," I spouted. "And I'd love to make some waves. So if any of you know people to whom I might want to talk, let me know."

There was some mumbling and snorting, but very little eye contact. I wasn't surprised; and it would probably be better all around if I didn't get any of my local chums involved.

A couple of days later, one of my buddies found me in the hotel lobby and put his arm around my shoulder. "I think we'd better have a little talk," he said.

It turned out, of course, that half the people I knew had become directly involved in smuggling in one way or another. To make matters worse, the Big Man About Lhasa had gotten wind of what I was planning. He wanted, it seemed, to have a little tête-à-tête with me.

My friend and I took the elevator up to the top floor of the Lhasa Hotel and walked down the hall to the room where the smuggler made his lair. It was an airy room, filled with beautiful work—all Tibetan. I admired his taste and told him so.

"Better we get it than the bastard Chinese," he said. "They'll just melt down whatever's gold and throw the rest into the fire."

There was a painful helping of truth in this. In many ways, I agreed with his point of view. Any artworks that remained in Tibet, anything of beauty or value, existed thanks to the fickle goodwill of the occupying Chinese. But my hasty assurance that the Mother Jones story would focus exclusively on the smuggling of devotional Nepalese art—as opposed to the lucrative trade out of Tibet—didn't seem to move him. The man had been in the business for a dozen years and maintained interdependent "offices" in both countries. As far as he was concerned, anyone who planned to draw attention to the smuggling trade at any level was an active menace to his livelihood.

We sat cross-legged on his balcony, warm and relaxed, the brilliant Lhasa sunshine glaring off the smuggler's pale, balding scalp. He was convivial, almost jolly, passing around hashish and good imported whiskey as we gossiped about the Chinese, the Tibetans, and the good money to be made in antique carpets. But the message he had called me up to deliver was out of tune with this veneer of bonhomie.

"I'm not threatening you," he said at last, merrily tapping a chunk of hash into a small water pipe. "But I advise you stay away from the art-smuggling story, and save yourself a pair of broken kneecaps—at *best*. Those Khampas are big men," he whispered, leaning forward. He was referring to the fierce nomads from Kham, eastern Tibet, who are apparently enriched by the trade. "And they can do a lot of damage."

This word to the wise, needless to say, had a curdling effect on my enthusiasm for the story. I mean, I'm concerned with the art theft problem, but not fanatic about it. So when I got back to Kathmandu, I put the art-smuggling story assignment on the back burner and tried to forget about it. But I couldn't forget it entirely, and toward the last month of my stay I again began to make discreet inquiries. I wasn't about to risk life and limb by writing a full exposé, but I figured I could get far enough to see how bad the problem really was, determine how the stealing was done, and at least issue a general bulletin about the phenomenon.

Bhaktapur, former home of the stolen Laksmi/Narayan statue, is a gem of a village located some 8 kilometers due east of Kathmandu. On clear autumn days, the Langtang Himalayas frame the city's tiered pagodas and temple finials like a cinematic backdrop—and it's possible to imagine Bhaktapur as it must have appeared hundreds of years ago, when it was the wood- and stone-carving capital of Central Asia.

Bhaktapur is where you'll find what's left of the flavor of old Kathmandu. Cars have to squeeze single file down the narrow alleys; little kids play bare-assed in front of rickety buildings. I wandered down the parquet brickwork of the ancient streets, searching for Jim Goodman—a man who, I'd heard, might shed some light on the art-smuggling scene in Kathmandu.

Entering the old Palace Square, I was surprised to encounter an enormous mob. A seething doughnut of humanity stood massed around the front steps of the Nyatapola, Bhaktapur's tallest and most famous pagoda. Standing on tiptoe, I heard muted drums and cymbals, followed by the unlikely bark of a bullhorn.

The man next to me, who had apparently been drawn into the crowd while heading home from both work and dinner shopping, hopped up and down for a better look. He was clutching a portable typewriter under one arm and a live chicken under the other. "Oh *daju*," I asked, "*Kay bayo?*" What's happenin'?

"*Movie gardaiccha!*"

Sure enough. The crowd was mesmerized by the filming of a made-for-television extravaganza, *Night Train to Kathmandu*. Never mind that there are no trains in Nepal whatsoever. I waded into the crowd and got a look at the action: blonde American kid-actors in LaCoste T-shirts posed in saucer-eyed disbelief, surrounded by a troupe of ethnic dancers wearing papier-mâché masks. A few steps away, barefoot local ragamuffins had abandoned their begging to gape at the Panavision cameras.

Several minutes after quitting that scene I came upon my destination. Goodman's house sat behind a large community washing area. It was a busy time of day; dozens of Nepalis squatted around the rectangular tank's perimeter, bathing, brushing their teeth, or beating their laundry.

After creeping up a deadly narrow stairway to the second floor, twice knocking my head on the low beams, I found Goodman in his parlor sorting through a bunch of color slides. He had longish blond hair and evasive eyes—or so it seemed at the start. And not surprisingly. Telephones are rare among fringe-dwelling expatriates, and Goodman was not among the privileged. As far as he was concerned, I was a total stranger, dropping in out of nowhere.

After satisfying himself that I wasn't the harbinger of any trouble (Goodman, like much of the foreign community, lived in continual terror of losing his visa and finding himself an instant persona non grata) Goodman loosened up and told me a bit about himself. He had stumbled across the art theft problem more or less by accident—returning to rephotograph certain temples for books and magazines, only to find them looted.

"It's become very embarrassing for me," he said, "to take people around Bhaktapur and show them empty niches where there were once great statues. And it's gotten worse; before, people used to take just the valuable things. Now they'll steal almost anything, just as an investment."

Jim led me on a walking tour of the city, and I could see what he meant. The most obvious victims were old *toranas*, ornate arches of metal or wood, which are installed above the entrances to temples all over the Kathmandu Valley. Described by one scholar as "iconographic blueprints," the toranas display, in miniature, figures of the gods and goddesses that appear inside the temple itself. The ones Goodman showed me were practically bare, stripped of all detail. Within the year, he predicted, the naked borders themselves would be ripped off.

In an awkward attempt to frustrate thieves, the more important shrines and statues are now being trussed up with barbed wire or caged behind metal grills—effectively preventing pilgrims from touching the images and receiving blessings in the traditional manner. It's a tactic that reminded me of how certain countries with scandalous rape statistics "solve" the problem by forbidding women to go out on the streets at night. And despite these clumsy measures, needless to say, the devotional figures continue to vanish at a fantastic rate.

Many of the stolen works are fairly small; they can easily be carried out of town in a daypack. But some are massive, requiring up to twenty men to lift. "I don't see how they get them out unnoticed," Goodman said. "The one downstairs from my flat—a very large sculpture of the god Shiva and his consort Parvati—was stolen twice. It was brought back the first time, but they couldn't convince the local people to put a cage around it. They thought that the power of the goddess brought it back." Within two weeks it was gone again—this time for good.

Hacking huge idols out of temples is not a quiet sport. Goodman mentioned that one Nepali reporter, investigating the thefts, theorized that gangs of looters disguise themselves as worshipers and enter the temples as if for a late-night puja—with horns, cymbals, and drums.

"They pretend to be celebrants—but in reality it's 'BOOM BOOM!' (chip, chip!), 'BOOM BOOM!' (chip, chip!)."

The encounter with Jim Goodman—and my stroll through Bhaktapur—was enough to convince me that any Buddha I finally did buy would have to be of recent origin. But the more I shopped around, the more disheartened I became. I could start to see why people who really loved the work, as paradoxical as this might sound, were inclined to

94

steal it. Once you've seen how beautiful a work of devotional art can be, it's hard to settle for a fifth-generation copy.

And so, confronting the generally low quality of all the contemporary Buddhas, my interest in antiquities became, let's say, piqued. I wanted to at least *see* what was possible, even if I wouldn't actually buy an illicit statue.

I'd heard about a shop called the Chandrama ("Moonlight") Gallery, just a hop and skip past the American Express mail stop and right next to a funky little Italian restaurant I had regularly patronized until finding a nine-inch length of high-gauge wire buried in my spinach ravioli one day. Just out of curiosity, I stopped in to the Chandrama to have a look-see.

All right, all right: I breached the bounds of pure, mindful Buddhist integrity. After a moment or two of browsing, I informed the manager that I was the Chief Curator of Nepalese and Indian Art for a major metropolitan U.S. museum, yes indeed, with my hands on a fabulous budget for, ahem, *antique* objects, if he knew what I meant. Might he have anything interesting to show me?

He began by offering up a few small statues that were obviously of very little real importance—and I told him so. A minute later I was sitting in the back room, surveying a table covered with seventeenth-century bronzes. I inquired about a seated Shiva, his hand cupping the breast of a voluptuous Parvati and was told that the price was 35,000 rupees, plus another 10,000 to ease it through customs: a total, in those days, of about $1,800.

When I pressed him for further rarities, the shop owner fetched a folio from the shelf and pulled out a snapshot of an old wood carving that he was safeguarding at home.

It was, as Goodman had predicted, a wooden torana—neatly stripped from a Bhaktapur temple.

13

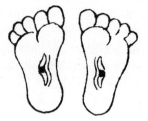

Nepal has a reputation for being a kind of Shangri-La; most people who visit—the average stay is only a week or two—don't have any need or desire to look behind the mask and notice such problems as art theft or human rights abuses.

A friend of mine working as a psychotherapist in Kathmandu remarked to me one evening that people visiting Nepal behave exactly as if they were having a love affair with a human being. They become giddy and intoxicated, seeing only the exoticism and mystery; as if their critical faculty had somehow been suspended.

"Or like a person on drugs," my friend said, "who is wandering through the jungle; and suddenly a tiger leaps out of the bush, right at them, and they scream, 'Oh, my God! What gorgeous green eyes!'"

Perhaps he was right—literally. Maybe a holiday to Nepal, a sudden and complete immersion into the stewpot of simmering human funk and fragrance, actually does something *physical* to your body and releases an enzyme into your bloodstream that makes everything seem so much more lush, more beautiful, more poignant. . . .

But Nepal is not Shangri-La. This became quite clear to me one afternoon as, between shopping bouts, I sat in the garden of the Kathmandu Guest House and read through an Amnesty International report entitled *Nepal: A Pattern of Human Rights Abuses*. Reading the booklet gave me a nagging sense of disconnection from the immediate environment, which consisted mainly of Western tourists and travelers lounging around on the manicured lawn, drinking fresh lemon sodas, reading travel guides, smoking hashish or Yak cigarettes, and reminiscing about the Hill Tribes of Thailand or the beaches at Goa. . . .

What, exactly, are the dynamics of responsible travel in the late twentieth century? Is a part of it knowing, *insisting* on knowing, about the human rights situation of countries that one visits for vacation? Do Americans *deserve* a vacation from that kind of information? The more I read of the Amnesty report, the more I felt an almost overpowering urge to climb up on a soapbox—to let everyone in that garden know exactly what I was reading, to ask questions about it, to become informed, outraged, active.

Instead I climbed up to the hotel's roof and read, alone, about torture, disappearances, pins under the fingernails, chili peppers up the ass, pausing every now and again to gaze northward toward the parade of shark-tooth Himalayas, or out over the hazy skyline of brick buildings toward the Royal Palace. The Amnesty report grated harshly against the Nepal I wanted to believe in: the magical land of incense and Buddha eyes, tea shops by the river, vermilion-smeared stone carvings of the Goddess of Compassion.

During the next week, I became increasingly curious about this hidden aspect of Nepal—the world of royal privilege, political intrigue, and human rights abuses that exists in the shadows of the sacred mountains. I began to make phone calls and arrange interviews, bent on finding out just how widespread and pervasive Amnesty International's charges were.

The first person I approached with my questions, a droll and insightful Nepali businessman who had been observing the political scene for nearly half a century, laughed out loud when I expressed my interest in investigating the kinds of abuses described in the Amnesty report.

"Human rights in Nepal," he declared, "is a square peg in a round hole. The entire thing is alien to the Hindu concept. In the Hindu world, you see, the loyalty is to family, clan, group. You do your duty as part of a group. You do your duty! Human rights, on the other hand, involves a conception of the individual: a single person, who can stand alone against the rest of society and the state."

He removed his glasses and began to polish them with the corner of a yellow handkerchief.

"Nepal is a hierarchical, caste-based society, based on exploitation. We are a Hindu kingdom. We swear by the Manusmriti: the Code of Manu, the Hindu religious code, written some five hundred years before Christ. And do you know what it says? 'Do not let the producing classes, the lowest castes, accumulate wealth. Dispossess them of their wealth as soon as they may gain it. They are there to serve the higher-caste people.'

"This very mentality," the businessman lamented, "works behind the scenes. It explains many policies, practices, and attitudes of the government, which consists mostly of appointed members from the higher castes.

"So never mind how you apply a veneer of Western political thought to the situation you find in Nepal! Our way of thinking remains traditionally Hindu."

The next afternoon I taxied up Lazimpat to the unwelcoming gates of the United States Embassy. If paranoia were a virus, this would be the petri dish to breed it in. Video cameras and body scans at the front gate; multiple, narrow-eyed telephone calls from the Nepali guards to their superiors deep inside the castle keep; the cardboard Marine guard at the reception area, ensconced behind a myopic thickness of bullet-proof, grenade-proof, humanity-proof glass. One states one's business and obeys orders. I was instructed to retire to the stark waiting room. The only diversion in that relentlessly functional purgatory was a copy of *State*, the State Department's anemic house organ, which lay on a thinly veneered table directly under a cheesy portrait of the president of the United States.

Richard March, the embassy official charged with keeping track of people like myself, entered the room through an armored door and greeted me. He possessed the classic, fade-away anonymity of a Le Carré spy. A narrow man, March was dressed almost completely in gray, which added to my impression that he was deeply and fundamentally uncomfortable; a bit drained around the edges, as if his body had recently become a stomping ground for microorganisms.

March led me upstairs. Every room looked self-consciously official, and inexplicably weary; as if the whole place had been designed as a set for a TV miniseries about Washington intrigue and backbiting. March himself, whom I quickly pegged as a basically harmless and well-meaning chap who spent most of his free time wondering what the hell he was doing in Nepal, found his complete physical opposite in Roy West, the beefy, cigar-puffing interim ambassador, who sat enthroned on a bulging Naugahyde couch in an appropriately intimidating office.

One never knows how frank diplomats are being. It's the nature of their business to be obtuse. But West was, as he readily admitted, "a bit to the right of center." He basically felt that the situation in Nepal was really no worse than the situation in, say, Mexico.

"The problem of King Birendra's lack of personal willpower is something that all of us have been hearing about lately. There's no doubt that people have become more and more outspoken, particularly over the past two or three years. You hear a lot of criticism of the government, of the system, and, after a scotch or two, about the king himself. Usually those kinds of statements have reflected more sorrow than anger; but maybe these days we're hearing more anger than sorrow. And they imply that the king is basically a well-intentioned, but perhaps ineffectual, man."

"It's hard being a king," March interjected. "It's hard breaking out of the shell. You create it, and the people around you create it."

When I asked directly about human rights, West said there was nothing unique about Nepal. "It's not very good—it's a system of limits. Within those limits, which are tolerably broad, you can get away with almost anything. Go a step beyond them, and you're in the slammer."

"The list of countries that live up to our standards," he added wryly, "is a very short list. . ."

"There are a lot of things about this kingdom that are extremely restrictive. Under the Public Security Act, you can arrest any Nepali citizen and put him or her away for nine months before charges have to be filed; eighteen months, if the order is imposed by the central government. And then, after you let them out, you can immediately *re-arrest* them a day or two later. It's very hard to claim the right not to be in prison if the government wants you in prison. And I've heard too many allegations of torture not to believe some of them."

"Anybody taken to jail around here gets beaten up," March added. "This is the procedure: you take somebody in, whether it's a pickpocket or whatever, you beat them up and get a confession. They don't do it to foreigners or to people who are socially prominent, but to everyone else."

"I'm not talking about beatings," West said. "I'm talking about torture: the deliberate infliction of pain, physical and/ or psychological, to extract information."

The tactics of the ruling class, it seems, sometimes go beyond even torture. One person who both March and West suggested I speak to was a journalist named Padam Thakurathi, an outspoken critic of government corruption who had recently—and miraculously—survived an assassination attempt at point-blank range.

"He would be a perfect person for you to talk to. That is, if he *feels* like talking to you. He's been considerably more subdued since the shooting.

"And by the way: be prepared," March added, shuddering. "I hope you're not too squeamish, because he was pretty horribly mutilated by the whole thing."

I left the embassy, emerging, molelike, onto the assaultive landscape of Lazimpat Road. For a moment I could hardly remember where I was. Then I mounted my bicycle and pedaled home, infected with an irresistible sense of purpose.

One of the great things about Nepal is that almost everybody, with the obvious exception of members of the royal family, is easily accessible. Thakurathi was one of the great opposition figures in Nepal, but it took me less than fifteen minutes to find his phone number, call him at home, and invite him over for lunch. He agreed to come a little later in the week.

14

I finished a cup of Sumatran coffee (Krishna had lobbed some whipped cream onto it, left over from last night's pumpkin pie) and checked warily on the crow. It was truly hideous; just looking at it was a serious threat to my mental health. It dangled by a thread, the once-meaty drumsticks down to white bone, yet the talons still miraculously grasping! Please, please let it fall! Let fall the abomination, and be done with it! I shuddered. Only a matter of days now. . . .

Another day, another shopping spree. I wheeled my Hero bicycle outside our gate to confront the latest in an ongoing series of municipal nightmares: cumulus clouds of choking dust, and a fusillade of apocalyptic roars as truckload after truckload of coarse gravel was dumped onto the roadway right in front of our little garden compound.

I groped, half-blinded, through a universe of chalky, abrasive powder, my hacking cough matched by a burning sense of embarrassment as I recalled my innocent lover's recently ended, ill-omened visit.

For months, Karen had been regaled with stories about the incomparably exotic charms of Nepal: its quaint streets, unpretentious lifestyle, and easy pace. But the Kathmandu she finally landed in whined an ugly contradiction to these psalms of praise. Throughout the entire length of her stay, His Majesty's Government was embroiled in a titanic effort to modernize Kathmandu. The process included paving miles of dirt roads, installing traffic lights, lathering the temples with fresh coats of paint and generally flinging about millions upon millions of rupees for cosmetic surgery. So intense was this zeal for modernization that many funky old homes—some of which had stood for centuries, surviving even the disastrous earthquake of 1934—were being razed to the ground (or literally cut in half) to make way for the broader avenues.

The speed and no-nonsense efficiency of the whole process was unprecedented, leading me to suspect that these were not your standard municipal improvements. Indeed, a few queries had revealed a very specific method to the madness. In early November, a major international conference (known by the acronym SAARC, for South Asian Association for Regional Cooperation) was scheduled to take place in Kathmandu. SAARC (pronounced "shark" by the disgusted Nepalis whose homes and neighborhoods had been gobbled up in the course of the city beautification program) was to be the first multinational political event ever hosted by the Kingdom of Nepal. Heads of state from India, Pakistan, Bhutan, Sri Lanka, and the Maldives would soon be conglomerating in the capital for casual, convivial chats. This was a landmark occasion, and no expense was being spared to give these cabbages and kings a convincing illusion of how truly advanced, how marvelously cosmopolitan little Kathmandu had become.

Karen and I had beat an escape from the city and trekked up to the sacred lakes at Gosainkund—that fateful trip—but it was just a temporary measure. The facelift was still in full swing when we returned and continued so—right up to the moment when Karen boarded her homeward-bound flight. Her memories of "Dreamland Nepal," I sadly realized, would always be dominated by violent images of backhoes, steam-rollers, and cement mixers.

By now, at the eleventh hour, the "improvements" had expanded to a level far beyond a simple revamp of the city's surface area. I noted, as I bicycled down the street, that all the familiar cripples, the ragged men who scoot around on little carts or pull themselves along the ground on pieces of tire rubber, were mysteriously absent. They'd been "relocat-ed," I was informed—but to where? And where were the infamous rickshaws, with their barefoot drivers, garishly painted cabs, and pathetically skewed awnings? Had they, too, like that ill-fated car within eyeshot of the king's motor-cade, been taken off to some "lonely place"?

The cows of course remained; but even they seemed somehow manicured, deodorized, and freshly shampooed. It was as if the entire city were being given a gigantic enema! Up and down the sidewalk in front of the Royal Palace, men on tottering ladders, their arms soaked to the elbow with silver (lead-based?) enamel were smearing paint all over the high, spiked fence that protects the beloved king and queen from their loyal subjects. . . .

As I pedaled along the eerily tidy avenues, I found my-self thinking about the legend of Buddha's youth. When Prince Siddhartha was born, the court astrologers instructed his father—King Suddhodana—to virtually imprison the prince in the palace and prevent the boy (at all costs!) from laying eyes on old people, sick people, dead people, or holy mendicants. The prince had all the marks of a divine king, Suddhodana was told; but if the boy ever beheld these baf-fling illustrations of the human condition, his extraordinary temperament would drown him in a maelstrom of compas-sion. The young prince would renounce everything—his family, his kingdom, the works—and wander off to seek the true causes of human suffering.

No wonder, then, that Kathmandu was being swept clean! No wonder flatbed trucks were rolling down the streets, full of bucket brigades who threw pails of whitewash over walls, garbage mounds, flowers, fences, trees, and dogs! No wonder the homeless, cripples, and itinerant *saddhus* had been shooed into the woodwork! These awful truths of human existence had to be kept hidden at all costs—for what limit to the apocalyptic renunciations that might ensue if any of these great Asian leaders glimpsed what life was like outside the palace gates??

The morning that Padam Thakurathi was due to arrive, I did some research. The journalist had been involved with one newspaper, which was shut down for criticizing His Majesty's Government. He then began *Bimarsha,* a weekly that focused on hard-hitting investigative reporting.

In 1976, there were about five hundred heroin addicts in Kathmandu. By the late 1980s, that number had exploded to over 15,000. Exactly how these boatloads of hard drugs were making their way into tightly controlled and geographically landlocked Nepal was a multimillion-rupee question, the answer to which was suspected by many, but verbalized by very, very few. In 1986, Thakurathi's paper started publishing a two-part exposé on the direct relationship between Nepal's skyrocketing heroin problem and the king's two brothers: Prince Gyanendra and Prince Direndra. It was that story, specifically, that very nearly cost Padam Thakurathi his life.

Thakurathi arrived on the dot of 11 A.M. on the appointed day, parking his bicycle on the front lawn. I finished brushing my teeth and let him in. The journalist was formally dressed, wearing a pale blue *daura surwal*—Nepal's traditional two-piece suit—under a sports jacket. A colorful green and orange topi, patterned with an abstract rhododendron motif, gave a splash of color to the outfit. His right eye—the artificial one—gazed morosely downward, but his living left eye was direct and convivial.

I saw no sign of the disfiguration that Richard March, the U.S. Embassy official, had mentioned; no "horrible mutilation." Thirty minutes into the interview, though, Thakurathi gave me a measuring glance. He then casually lifted off his topi, and I saw at once what March had meant.

The upper right portion of the journalist's skull, from just above the eyebrow to high up the scalp, was . . . *missing.* The skin simply caved in, following the shape of a huge, craterlike depression that seems to have eaten up a good 30 percent of his frontal lobes. It looked for all the world like the surgeons had gone at him with an ice cream scoop.

Thakurathi's survival was a double miracle. Not only did the journalist live; he has apparently retained all his incisive mental functions. Although Thakurathi spoke slowly and with great deliberation, he immediately disproved March's theory that he would be subdued and reluctant.

I asked Thakurathi if he felt capable of recalling the events leading up to the assassination attempt itself. He agreed without hesitation.

"I had nothing; no suspicion in my mind. The very day the shooting took place, I was participating in a journalists' conference that lasted from morning to evening. From that meeting, I came back home and took my family to a friend's house. We had been asked for a dinner there. And then we came back to our house and went to bed.

"I have no memory of anything happening until thirty-five days later, when I regained consciousness in Samiti Vej Hospital in Bangkok."

Thakurathi has pieced together the events that followed immediately after the shooting. His wife had been sleeping with him; when she heard the sound of the gun she jumped from the bed and threw on the light—nearly fainting from what she saw. Her husband's right eye had been blown from its socket, and the cotton mattress was saturated with blood. She ran from the house and called the neighbors, who helped get the journalist to a local hospital.

But the Kathmandu facilities were inadequate to his grievous wound. Fortunately, Thakurathi—himself a former member of the National Assembly—had friends in high places. An official order directed that he be flown to the more sophisticated operating theaters in Bangkok.

I remarked that God must have been on his side, for him to have lived.

"Yes. That is the only factor that I lived—because of God. My doctor told me that, in all the years of his practice, he had never witnessed such a miracle."

In late 1986, there was a huge and unprecedented crackdown in Kathmandu. Many of the slimiest officials, including the inspector general of police and Prince Direndra's aide-de-camp, were arrested and eventually given long prison sentences. I asked Thakurathi if these measures had lessened the corruption problem in Nepal.

"No, no, no. It has not even been touched. There are a few people who have been taken, but the organizers of the corruption and drug trafficking are still running freely. Mostly they are the people from the Royal Palace: the secretaries, and the king's brothers—both of them, until recently. Earlier this year, you see, Direndra left the country. For good, I think."

"Why was that?"

"Well, because he was defaming the royal family with his actions. There was his involvement in things like my case, and things like drug trafficking and gold smuggling. So he was made to leave. The news given to the people was that he had resigned his post, but it was a forced resignation."

"So that leaves only Gyanendra. Are things just as bad as they were before?"

"Yes."

"I find that hard to believe," I said, "because, as you know, Prince Gyanendra has an international reputation as a great conservationist. He's the chairman of the Lumbini Development Project and the King Mahendra Trust for Nature Conservation. He even gave two baby rhinos to the San Francisco Zoo!"

Thakurathi gazed at me sardonically with his left eye; his right seemed to trace the weave of the cotton tablecloth. "That's only show business," he said. "Gyanendra is the main link to the international drug traffickers. We have come to know this through discussions with very reliable sources: the people who worked closely with him. Certain people in prison have made statements."

This evidence seemed circumstantial at best, and I told Thakurathi so. But both he and the other insiders I would eventually speak with laughed off my doubts and regarded me as if I were astonishingly dense. It was all a matter of logic, they said. It *had* to be the royal family. How could anyone else get away with it? Nepal is a small country; the Kathmandu Valley, where the vast majority of the addicts live, is even smaller. Nepal is a word-of-mouth society; everybody knows what everybody else is up to. If a thriving, multimillion-rupee business in heroin and brown sugar is being tolerated, it can only be because the highest people in the know—the *very* highest—are either in direct control or receiving an extraordinary cut.

"You're giving me the impression, Mr. Thakurathi, that members of the royal family are basically immune from criminal charges no matter what laws they break."

"Yes! That's right!" He gave me the look that a teacher gives to an average student who surprises him with a moment of insight. "Mr. Bharat Gurung was the aide-de-camp, the bodyguard of Direndra. He was caught, tried, and penalized for the crime of trying to kill me. But as I was told by some of the people who were in custody along with him, he kept saying that he had just carried out the order to kill me—an order that was given to him by Prince Direndra."

"Bharat Gurung," I said, "was sentenced to thirty-three years in prison and millions of rupees in fines. I'm surprised he hasn't come right out and pointed the finger directly at Prince Direndra, if it was he who gave the order to assassinate you."

"It is the police who have to take the statements. And the police won't mention the prince's name." Thakurathi laughed without bitterness. "Even if Gurung says the prince told him to do it, it won't be reported."

"So were both the princes involved in these illegal activities?"

"Oh, yes. They are equally responsible. Especially in the gold smuggling. According to the law of Nepal, customs officers are not authorized to check their baggage. They travel in an entourage and can smuggle in any amount of gold or heroin. This gang has been doing all sorts of things, including the art smuggling. As I was told by their contractors: they bring the drugs in from Thailand and there are some agents here. Some of them were caught in 1987, along with the others."

"Does the king know what his brothers are doing?"

"He must know. I had a chance to meet with His Majesty two or three years back. I told him, 'Your brothers are involved with such business, and to save your own image you must act quickly.' He said, 'I will see.'"

Thakurathi sipped at his water for a moment. "I don't know," he said. "I think in that family he has little say. I think they decide everything in family meetings."

"Okay—so what if your paper was to publish a story that said it was Direndra who ordered Gurung to shoot you?"

"We cannot publish like that. We will be arrested, and our paper will be seized. Canceled."

"So what can you do?" I wondered out loud. "Nepal's problems seem to be directly connected to the Royal Palace. How can you keep hammering away at them if it's against the law for you to implicate the royal family?"

"We will be publishing as much as we can. We will make the people conscious of what's going on in the country. I'm not afraid. I will continue on with my work."

I asked Thakurathi if he had seen the Amnesty International report. He said he had indeed gotten hold of one, although copies were, predictably, difficult to come by in Nepal.

"The report is perfectly correct," he said. "In October of 1987, I was taken into custody for a story I wrote about the milk scandal. It was claimed that the Government Dairy Board was buying cheap powdered milk from Poland that had been contaminated by the Chernobyl fallout.

"During my twenty-five days in prison, I saw a person who was taken in, seven hours a day, for beatings. They beat him on the soles of the feet, and on the whole body. When he used to come back from the beatings, he was not able to walk. And I saw so many cases of burning from the cigarettes. The police wanted a false statement from him, a confession, that he had stolen sacred art from the temples."

"Had he really stolen the art?"

"No."

"Then why were they beating him?"

"I don't know," said Thakurathi. "There was nothing. I think they wanted to use him as a scapegoat. They wanted a confession. In Nepal, most of the cases are decided on such statements. To get that statement, they used to beat him seven hours a day. But they never got it. Perhaps he is still in prison."

There was a long silence. Thakurathi took a small packet of Pan Parag, an herbal chew, from his jacket pocket and popped a few of the pungent granules into his mouth.

I refilled our water glasses. My mind wandered. The story about the beatings in prison was dramatic and deplorable, but I found myself thinking about human rights on a much larger scale. Nepal is one of the world's poorest countries; the average per capita income is something like $160 a year. For most Nepalis—the vast population of subsistence farmers who live outside of the Kathmandu Valley—life is a continual struggle against a host of problems: deforestation and erosion, malnutrition and disease, population pressure, bad drinking water, illiteracy. All over Nepal, the basic needs of millions of people remain unmet. Meanwhile, journalists who try to bring these issues into public debate—people like Thakurathi—are hauled into prison for expressing their views.

"Nepal is obviously in trouble," I said. "But millions on millions of dollars in development money is constantly pouring in from foreign sources—Japan, China, Europe, the United States, the Soviet Union, the World Bank. Isn't it helping? I mean, do you think the situation for the average person in Nepal, the people who live up in the hills, is getting better?"

"It's getting worse. Because the foreign aid is being distributed among a few families. Very little goes to the areas for which it has been asked. All the officers and project chiefs are nominated according to the wishes of the Royal Palace.

"Do you think," I asked helplessly, "that there's any hope for a change here in the near future? Is there any way that things will get better?"

"I don't think so. Because the king is so powerful. The army and police are very much behind the king. And that is the only base of his rule."

Thakurathi agreed with the conventional wisdom that the king is a decent human being surrounded by very bad advisors. "During that period of time when I was in the Rastriya Panchayat, I had the opportunity to talk with him. In person. And I received the impression that he is truly worried about the development of the country. But he's not decisive enough. He can't make the right decision at the right moment."

The tragic irony of the whole situation, I felt, is that Nepal has a constitution that ostensibly provides for law, order, and basic human rights. But unlike the Constitution of the United States, which originated "Of the people, by the people and for the people," Nepal's constitution is a gift from the king—who can revoke it at any time.

"There is one proverb in Nepali," Thakurathi told me. "'The elephant has the teeth outside: they are only to show, not to eat.' And so, in Nepal, the constitution is just like those tusks: only for show."

Listening to Thakurathi's reflections on Nepal's crisis of leadership, I was reminded of a story that I'd heard at a dinner party a couple of weeks before.

All over Nepal—"the World's Only Hindu Kingdom"—cows are revered as sacred. It is a Hindu belief that cows are the reincarnations of beloved relatives; allies who play a crucial role in the cycle of existence by leading recently deceased family members—who, blind and terrified, cling desperately to their tails—across the dread Rivers of Fire that lie between death and the afterlife.

Cows are given the run of Kathmandu. Festivals honor them; passers-by touch them for a blessing; vegetable vendors throw wilting spinach and carrots to them. I once watched an old woman stand behind a cow in a courtyard, collecting its sacred dung in her hands before the steaming mass had a chance to hit the ground.

Bovines of all colors and sizes are often seen lounging about the roads and sidewalks, chewing their cuds as traffic swerves around them. And swerve it must: to injure a cow is a criminal offense, and drivers who inadvertently hit and kill the animals have sometimes been lynched right on the spot.

All this just to relate a brief anecdote about an occasion where a truck had to unload some crates in front of a shop where a cow had settled herself for the afternoon. The driver tried honking; tried shouting; tried pushing. No avail. Finally he figured he'd just nudge the cow with the vehicle and get it on its way. But the bovine wouldn't budge—it stayed right where it was even as the truck crushed its leg.

It seemed a perfect allegory. Cows are sacred—why should they move just because they're being pushed? Especially if the one doing the pushing can be thrown into prison on a whim. The monarchy is, to some extent, like those sacred cows. It may be blocking the smooth flow of traffic (er, ideas), but the entire system has evolved to respect its inviolable right to immobility.

15

Human desires are endless. It is like the thirst of a man
who drinks salt water: he gets no satisfaction and his
thirst is only increased.

—BUKKYO DENDO KYOKAI, *The Teaching of Buddha*

Every time I go shopping in Nepal I encounter an array of
objects as fascinating as crib toys. You remember: those marvelous, colorful busy-boxes that gave us our first lessons
about shape and color and sound and prepared us for the
intimidating world of eye-hand coordination. In my more
enlightened moments, I begin to realize that everything the
adult world plays with is just an extension of the crib toy.

Wandering through the streets of Patan's Durbar Square
in search of an elegant bronze statue, flying high on a few
light puffs of eye-opening Nepali hash, I was able to recall
the flavor of that enviable infant attention span.

It was in this frame of mind that I espied, in an out-of-
the-way little shop, a handsome bronze statue of Chenrezig.

Chenrezig, like Tara, is a bodhisattva of compassion. His
beat is Tibet; the line of Dalai Lamas is believed to be the
direct human manifestation of Chenrezig, tirelessly striving
for the liberation of all sentient beings—cats, puffer-fish,
ants, camels, lawyers—on earth. South of the Himalayas,
Chenrezig wears a lighter outfit and is caught performing

different asanas and mudras; in Nepal, he usually goes by the Sanskrit name of Avalokiteshwara. As Nepal is the Land of Ten Thousand Gods, consummately catholic in its esthetic and devotional tastes, it was not the least bit surprising to run into the patron deity of the Tibetan highlands in a Patan curio shop.

The shopkeeper noticed that I was admiring the statue and took it from the display case. He set it on the counter and traced its perfectly symmetrical outline with his hands.

"Can you see," the merchant asked, "that Chenrezig's meditating body is imitating the shape of a bell? In our Tibetan religion, the bell—we call it *drilbu*—is the shape for compassion. Compassion and wisdom, united together, mean enlightenment. So Chenrezig, you see, being bodhisattva of compassion, is shaped like the bell."

"And what about wisdom?"

"Ah!" The shopkeeper lifted another statue from the case—one I readily recognized. "You see: this is Manjushri. He is holding the sword. This sword is like the shape of the *vajra*, what you call thunderbolt. It is the symbol of wisdom. Very bright; very powerful. Manjushri is shaped like this."

The Patan shopkeeper's ideas about the metaphorical shapes of his statues may have owed more to his own imagination than to any traditional teaching, but one element of his lesson clicked home. During Tibetan rituals, I had watched the high lamas grasp a drilbu in one hand and a stylized, two-pointed vajra in the other, swinging them toward each other while chanting the sutras. Now it all made sense: they were combining the two, blending wisdom and compassion, mixing up the recipe for enlightenment.

I continued my rounds in Patan, looking with new interest at the Chenrezigs in the various shops. None of them seemed nearly as good as the first one I had seen—not by a long shot. A leisurely survey through the markets of Kathmandu confirmed this impression, and within a few days the wonderful, terrible truth of the situation became clear to me.

I had made a find. An honest-to-goodness find. Mysterious glands began secreting their potent liquors into my bloodstream, compelling me to buy. My heartbeat began to quicken at the very mention of Chenrezig; my breath came in short, shallow gasps, as if I were recalling the face of a lover. No doubt about it: I was primed for the pounce. All I needed was a quick blessing from my hunting partner.

As soon as Nancy returned from her sojourn in the Chitwan jungle, I phoned the owner of the shop—Tashi was his name—and set a time for us to come and look at his Chenrezig again. At the appointed hour, Nancy and I hired a cab to drive us out to Patan.

Patan is a four- or five-mile ride out of Kathmandu, over the Bagmati River and up the hill. As we passed the river, we saw a poignant sight: a bright yellow dumpster, one of many recently installed as part of the Solid Waste Management Program, had been overturned by a group of street waifs and beggars. The foul contents had been scattered over the street and were being sifted for fruit rinds, tattered cardboard, and other scraps. Another ambitious gesture gone awry; I was certain that whatever foreign aid organization had donated these dumpsters to Nepal had not calculated that they would be the Third World equivalent of Goodwill depositories.

For the remainder of the ride to Patan, I talked up my once and future Chenrezig, recalling its perfect bell shape and swelling with conviction. At last, the cab dropped us off near the fabulous temples of the old Palace Square. We strolled past the pagodas, into the shopping district, through an ever-narrowing maze of alleyways until—right on time—we located Tashi's shop.

It was closed! Bright blue shutters boarded the windows, and a big, black Chinese "Friendship" brand padlock bolted the door. What to do? I muttered an awkward apology to Nancy and ran off to fetch some plain sodas. We planted ourselves on the step.

We waited; and waited. I started to get a little bit irritated. Where the hell was this guy, anyway? After another fifteen minutes I was a lot irritated. Who did this arrogant son of a bitch think I was? Nancy cleared her throat, and my badly stretched thread of good will snapped. Time, I determined, to adopt a somewhat more agressive strategy. Where, to begin with, did this clown live?

After asking around at the neighboring shops, we were directed to the sculptors' district. The setting was positively medieval. Dogs limped through the streets; thick smoke, tasting of rough tobacco and hot wax, plumed out of carved wooden windows. Clusters of pan-spitting twelve-year-old boys sat in some of the doorways, chain-smoking Yak filter cigarettes and laying into half-finished Buddhas, Taras, and Manjushris with primitive carving tools.

Our shopkeeper's house was a tall white structure that leaned imposingly into the narrow, brick-paved alley. I knocked at the rickety wooden door. No answer. Damnation! The guy wasn't even home! At last the sowji's little son answered the door and bade us wait inside.

"Where is your father?"

"Gone away. He come back soon, I think."

"How soon?"

The boy wagged his head noncommittally. I snorted. Time was a wastin'. Our appointment had been for two; it was already a quarter to four. Soon the shops down on New Road would be closed—their new shipments of Buddhas spoken for by affluent collectors. Who could say what golden opportunities were slipping away as we bided our time in Patan? Finally it was too much to stand.

"Tell your father I couldn't wait any longer," I said, "and that his rudeness has cost him a very important sale. I was genuinely interested in that little Chenrezig."

"You must please come back tomorrow."

"No chance. One wasted day is enough."

The moment we stood up to leave I heard the timpanic thrum of a motorcycle approaching down the alley. Sure enough, it was Tashi, the proprietor of the shop. He parked the cycle, glanced guiltily at me, and pulled off his helmet. He looked surprisingly pale.

"I'm sorry to be so late. . . ."

"I'm sorry too," I snapped.

" . . . but right after you called, my sister-in-law came running over to give me some terrible news. My brother was hit by a taxi, and they had to rush him to Patan Hospital."

"I see." We stood there in silence for a long moment. "Gee, I'm really sorry." More silence; it was still my move. "Well," I said, "do you feel like taking a walk down to your shop? I'd still like to see that Chenrezig."

The shopkeeper nodded, and we strolled in silence to his store. He opened the lock and threw back the shutters. There it was—the statue that I'd had such grand memories of—that I had essentially made up my mind to buy.

But wait! Something was wrong! Something was terribly, terribly wrong! The Chenrezig, which in my memory had been smooth and clean, seemed to be covered all over with black, rancid butter!

"What's all this gook?" I cried, setting the statue down and wiping my hands compulsively on my jeans. I turned to Nancy, embarrassed and apologetic. "It wasn't like this before!"

"Oh, yes," Tashi muttered. "Same, same, same. . . ."

"No it was *not* the same! What have you done? You've smeared all this butter oil all over it! Oh, why, why, why?"

"Same as before. Nothing is change."

I heaved a sigh of disappointment and shook my head. Was he right? No—couldn't be—I would definitely have remembered something like this! Wouldn't I?

"Well, listen. There must be some way to clean all this stuff off, isn't there? Some chemical? Look, I could do it myself."

The shopkeeper picked his keys up off the glass counter. I won't describe the look he gave me.

"There is no way. Everything is same. You see the bell shape? Same. So. Do you want to buy?"

"No. No. No. No."

I trudged from the shop into the dusty dry air, avoiding the sight of my reflection in the snack shop windowpanes.

My only thought, as I shuffled miserably down the street, was that if the Buddha himself had witnessed that scene he would have been horrified.

His reaction would have had little to do with the issue of my reaction to the news of Tashi's injured brother, or with the fact that I had been having fits over cooling my heels for a couple of hours. No—Buddha would have been bent out of shape by the irksome realization that here and now, a mere two-and-a-half millennia after his death, the most important of his unspoken lessons was being outrageously flaunted. Buddha was famous for his clarity, and there was a particular issue he seems to have been especially adamant about: he was not a God. Nor was he a saint, angel, deity, divine personage, heavenly host, or holy ghost. He was simply an awakened human being—species *Homo*, genus *sapiens*—who had found, and traveled, the Path.

This was the whole point. We could do it, too. Anyone can. You don't have to be a member of some celestial Bohemian Club.

Graven idols were completely anathema to the Buddha's philosophy. Not only didn't he approve of them, but anyone with any sense could see that they wouldn't do any good. There was no point to them. To achieve insight in meditation, one looks within. When you find the Buddha there, you know you're on the right track.

For five hundred odd years after his death, the Buddha's directive was respected. No likenesses of him were made (unless you count a couple of legendary ones, which I'll get to in a minute). There were, however, at least half a dozen ingenious ways of portraying the Buddha with symbols. There was the Bodhi tree (*Ficus religiosa*) with its long-tongued leaves, under which Siddhartha Gautama battled with Mara and found enlightenment; the lotus, the eternal lotus, whose heart-shaped bud explodes into a radiant natural mandala; the eight-spoked wheel, symbolizing the Law; the Buddha's footprints, displayed alone or in front of an empty throne; the stupa, which some say represents a retired, overturned, begging bowl; and the flaming pillar, ancient symbol of the link between heaven and earth.

Now, about those legends. The first concerns a ruler named King Udrayana, who supposedly lived during the time of Buddha. One day the king, a devout Buddhist himself, convinced himself, for variously described motives, that he required an effigy of his spiritual master. One version tells how Buddha was paying a courtesy call to heaven when Udrayana—Buddhism's first spiritual materialist—decided he missed the Buddha so badly that he had to have at least a statue of his absent teacher, and damn the expense. Udrayana dispatched a sculptor up to the celestial realm, and the artist returned with an exact sandalwood likeness. Some believe this statue actually exists. Needless to say, it has never turned up.

In another story we cast King Bimbisara, a contemporary of King Udrayana, as the patron of the arts. Bimbisara wanted to convert Udrayana to Buddhism and decided that the only way to do it was to present his royal chum with a portrait of the Buddha.

Buddha, we are to believe, agreed. He thought it was a great idea and instructed King Bimbisara's painters to bring along a large piece of silk. Early in the morning, the bolt of cloth was draped on one of the palace's outdoor walls. Buddha stood so that the rays of the rising sun threw his shadow directly onto the fabric and told the painters to trace his form exactly. He then dictated which colors were to be used and indicated which of his teachings were to be inscribed alongside the completed figure.

"As soon as King Udrayana sees this painting," the Buddha declared, "he will develop faith in my teachings and perceive the true nature of reality." This esthetic feat, we duly note, anticipated, by some twenty-five centuries, a somewhat less ambitious goal expressed by Pablo Picasso: "I wish to see art evolve to the point where a painting can cure a toothache."

Whether or not Udrayana existed, the fact remains that there just aren't any surviving Buddha images made earlier than the first century A.D.—at which point there was an obvious shift in the wind. Buddhism was spreading, like a flood of spilled honey, far beyond India's bustling hive. Artists influenced by the heroic traditions of the Greco-Roman school, working in the regions that we now call Iran, Afghanistan, and Pakistan, knew an open field when they saw one. They grabbed the Buddha ball and ran with it, producing images of a youthful, vital champion modeled after the classical heroes of Western mythology—especially Apollo, the sun god.

At the same time that this process was taking place, it was becoming disconcertingly clear—to people whose livelihoods depended on it—that feet, empty thrones, and even flaming pillars were not holding their ground against fantastic images of dancing elephants, grinning bulls, ferocious monkey-headed gods, blood-drinking demons, and melon-breasted river nymphs. People just couldn't identify with a wheel . . . and the virile and voluptuous deities of Hinduism were elbowing their way back into style. If Buddhism wanted to remain attractive to the large lay population of India, it had to bend.

Slowly, slowly, but in ever-increasing numbers, artisans lowered their defenses and began creating statues, paintings, and friezes of the Buddha in all his most famous and enchanting moments. They must have seemed overwhelmed by the possibilities; there was, after all, five hundred years of accumulated lore and legend that had been hiding gleefully in the shadows, anticipating its opportunity to burst upon the temples and altars, pillars and caves, mountainsides, monasteries and manuscripts that waited across the steaming breadth of Asia.

There was baby Siddhartha's conception, accompanied by Princess Maya's dream of a six-tusked white elephant; his miraculous birth, popping out of Mom's right side as she waited patiently in a grove; the Great Renunciation, when the prince snuck out of Kapilavastu Palace on his trusted steed, Kanthaka, vowing never to return until he had found "the Deathless State." There was the silent battle beneath the Bodhi tree, Buddha versus Mara, culminating in the moment of enlightenment; Buddha's first reluctant sermon in the Deer Park at Sarnath (the gods, it is said, had to pursuade him to teach); and everything in between that first lesson and the End: the Buddha reclining easily on his right side, giving a final pep talk to his monks before passing into nirvana at the ripe old age of eighty.

And all these scenes were drawn, and carved, and drawn again, over and over and over, all through the parade of years—across the reign of emperors and inquisitors and tzars, through the click-clacking lifetimes of astronomers and inventors and racing car drivers—until one day, late in the twentieth century, one basically well-meaning marsupial sahib stomped from a souvenir shop in Patan, leaving a fuming sowji behind.

While somewhere on high, in the golden cloudy realms of the Tushita Heaven, the Buddha himself—who knew well in advance about the various brands of grief that these images could and would cause—observes the situation with characteristic detachment, twines his fingers into the teaching mudra, and whispers,

. . . Even this dirty day will wash away. . . .

16

Nancy and Rick left Nepal at the beginning of December, attempting to get a running start on the riot of holiday festivities hosted by their respective families. They departed clear-headed and content, gleaming with fine memories, traveling light, and bringing home—as I was painfully aware—a nearly perfect, signed Sidhi Raj.

During the next few weeks, alone in Nepal, my life took on a frighteningly narrow focus. The only exercise I got was shopping for Buddhas; cycling maniacally downtown, zipping along recently paved and unnaturally broad roads and into the half-dozen shops that had become my veritable opium dens for the daily Buddha fix.

It was truly aerobic. My heart rate and adrenaline skyrocketed every time I threw back a curtain and walked into one of those dimly lit back rooms, hoping beyond hope that today, today, I'd find it—the Buddha of my Dreams, reasonably priced, beatific, of a decent size, with none of the galling flaws that seemed to crop up in Buddha after Buddha. Because even though I might agree to buy a filing cabinet with a few surface scratches, or take a discount on an irregular pair of sneakers, I somehow could not reconcile the thought of buying a seriously flawed Buddha—even for 10 percent off list. The whole concept seemed a loathesome compromise of the goal I had in mind: spending money generously and without regret for an object that had no real use in the occidental scheme of things.

For once in my life, I was going to buy retail.

And so, at last, after having eaten up uncounted hours with repeated visits to all the rest, I decided to try the best. I stopped in at the finest, most expensive art gallery in Kathmandu: the Oriental Art Emporium, owned by a black-eyed and cerebral young man named Babukaji.

To enter Babukaji's shop was to step into a world utterly removed from the familiar chaos of the ambient street scene. The impudent orchestra of New Road—shouting, honking, whistling, and mooing—faded into oblivion as I closed the door behind me. It was almost as if the interior of the gallery created a zone of silence around itself. I blinked, waiting for my brain to adjust to this subdued new esthetic.

Babukaji sat behind a wide desk cluttered with bills and letters. He was on the phone, speaking in imperative whispers, and nodded briefly to acknowledge my presence. It was impossible to guess his age; he could have been anywhere from twenty-one to forty-five.

Babukaji's shop seemed to combine the best qualities of both gallery and shrine. The artworks, displayed in polished and well-lit showcases, were extraordinary. I found my materialistic frenzy loosening, dissolving into puddles of reverence and supplication. I began to suspect what it would mean—in terms of *responsibility*—to own a truly potent work of devotional art.

There was a macabre Tibetan ritual cup, fashioned from the silver-lined cranium of a long-dead lama. . . .

There was an enormous bronze Tara, at least four centuries old, as lithe and athletic as an aerobics instructor. . . .

There was a fabulous bejeweled Manjushri, flaming sword held menacing and true, whose eyes seemed to follow me around the room. . . .

There was a gilt statue of Padmasambhava, the great mystic and magician who brought Buddhism to Tibet 1,200 years ago. The scepter in the saint's hand displayed three impaled heads, demonstrating the seer's complete mastery of the Three Realms of Existence. . . .

There were yogic saints and dancing Ganeshes; singing brass bowls and Tibetan bells made from long-forgotten alloys; prayer beads carved from human bones; ritual daggers with demonic faces engraved on their hilts.

There was everything anyone could possibly wish for, except a statue of the Buddha.

"How may I help you?"

Babukaji had ended his conversation and crept up silently behind me, catlike, catching me off guard. In a lame attempt to sound casual, I began to prattle uncontrollably.

"Well—gee, I don't know. You've got some beautiful stuff here, no doubt about it, but I'm frankly sort of disappointed by the selection. I mean, aren't you a bit short on Buddhas? After all, this is Nepal, Buddha was *born* here, so I guess I figured you'd have at least a couple of really topnotch statues; nothing sloppy, mind you, but a really sweet little—"

"Wait."

Babukaji raised his palm, and I screeched to a halt. "Allow me to show you something."

He walked behind a low display case, parted a maroon curtain, and vanished into a back room. I heard a drawer squeaking open; the jangle of keys; the snap of a lock; another creak. Then Babukaji reappeared, carrying a small parcel completely mummified in rice paper and tied with string—like a Nepali Maltese Falcon. He set it down on a countertop and removed the wrappings.

The chemistry was immediate, complete, and devastating.

For several minutes I could not speak. My ears were ringing; the shop seemed to go soft-focus around me. I felt like a kid at Christmas time, staring through a frosted windowpane at the Flexible Flyer of his dreams. Images of coasting fearlessly across the thin ice of this particular lifetime, my new Buddha by my side, danced giddily in my head. I dreamed of the ease and speed with which we would sleigh, the Buddha steering, around the stumps and moguls of samsara—illusion and suffering—that lay all along life's twisting path.

"I'll take it," I said.

There was a brief, strained silence. I turned around to face Babukaji and repeated my claim.

"I'm so sorry." The shopkeeper folded his hands and seemed to bow slightly. "But that particular Buddha is not for sale. It is by the hand of Sidhi Raj himself and is being held in reserve for a very important Japanese collector. Besides," he added gently, eyes glancing down at my tattered tennies, "I think maybe this one is a little too expensive for you."

This was the very moment that I'd been waiting for: the chance to cast off an entire childhood of operant conditioning with a single, devil-may-care gesture. A little smile crossed my lips. "Ah, c'mon, tell me. You might be surprised. How much?"

Babukaji smiled as well. "Fifteen thousand rupees," he said evenly.

My mouth dropped open. I barked out a laugh; there had to be a mistake. Numbers, I knew, were always a point of confusion for nonnative speakers.

"Write it down," I insisted. And he did, slowly and carefully: a 1, a 5, a comma, and three zeroes.

"Fifteen thousand rupees," he repeated.

I whipped out my pocket calculator and divided by 22.5, the going exchange rate.

"But—but—that comes to $666.66666! I'd have to be sick to spend that much money on a Buddha! Whew! Hey!" I slapped my forehead, feeling much like the fall guy in some dumb situation comedy. "You've got to be kidding!"

I paced around the shop as Babukaji rewrapped the statue, dividing the figures again and again in the hope that I had made some grievous error with the math. But no—that devilish row of 6's continued to display itself, with an impassivity that was itself almost Buddhalike, in the tiny liquid crystal display.

"Heh!" I croaked. The wisest thing to do, without a doubt, was to put this insane temptation behind me as quickly as possible.

But not quite yet.

"Listen," I muttered imploringly. "Let me just have one last look."

Babukaji did not blink an eye; he calmly unwrapped the Buddha once more and placed it in my hands. Although barely nine inches high it was, truly, a marvelous work of art. Babukaji knew; he knew that I knew. At one point I took a breath, right on the verge of bargaining. But when our eyes met, Babukaji gave his head the merest shake. It was sufficient; I said nothing.

The Nepalis have such beautiful features: so refined. So *sculpted*. After spending a month looking at statues, you re-

128

alize that everyone you see on the street resembles one of them. The university co-ed sitting sidesaddle on the back of her brother's motorcycle must have been the model for the Tara I'd passed up a couple of days ago; that rotund fellow lounging in the glass bead necklace stall could only be Ganesh; that little boy ringing the bell on his father's bicycle was the baby Krishna. . . .

Late at night, when I went to bed, I closed my eyes and still saw all those faces. But one face in particular kept creeping into my consciousness, insinuating itself into my dreams. It was the face of Babukaji's Buddha—all $666.66 worth.

And a damned good thing, I thought to myself miserably, that it wasn't for sale.

I returned to Babukaji's every day for a week, hoping he might get something else in, something even remotely comparable—and half the price—of that superb copper Buddha. Every day I asked to look at it again, and every day he patiently took it out of the back room, unwrapped it, and let me gaze at its perfect features.

One afternoon Babukaji said, "I must tell you something. I have learned, just yesterday, that this Japanese dealer has left town. He did not leave word with me, so I must assume he is abandoning this deal. And so I ask you: do you wish to buy this Buddha?"

I wheezed; I gulped; I asked the price, hoping beyond hope that Babukaji would have pity on the poor dollar. No chance; the price was fixed. By now, though, the rupee had slightly devalued. The Buddha would cost me $650, if I changed money on the black market.

"I gotta think about it," I pleaded.

"Yes," said Babukaji. "I will sell it to no one else until you have decided."

17

No matter what's going on in your life, if you walk down the streets in Kathmandu you'll run smack into a metaphor for it. That's what I love—and fear—most about Nepal.

I strolled down toward the Bagmati River, desperately confused. What to do? I was completely in love with that Buddha in Babukaji's shop—but $650! It was a mind-numbing figure. My car cost less than that!

My face felt pale and wan. When was the last time I spent $50 for a nice shirt? I mean, okay, $300 is an exercise, a deep breath that you have to take. A plunge. And it's true—staring at that $650 price tag I felt like one of those Nepalis who were standing by the side of the escalator, daring themselves to jump on, except that while the escalator was just a ride—and a *free* ride—this Buddha represented a small fortune. It cost far more than I earned during some of my leaner months as a writer.

Down at the river, the usual activities were in progress. People were bathing, washing their clothes, watering their buffaloes. I was just about to cross over the bridge to the other side when I saw something going on at a little temple by the bank. A man in a white breechcloth was sweeping,

sweeping, sweeping the ashes off of a circular pedestal, or *ghat*, upon which a cremation had just been completed.

At that moment I remembered something.

Months ago, while Karen was still visiting, we woke up early one morning and took a taxi out to Pashupatinath, a very important Shiva temple just east of the city. The temple grounds are bisected by the Bagmati River, which manifests directly from Shiva's scalp up in the western Himalayas. It follows a twisting course across the Tibetan Plateau, down into Nepal and south to India, where it joins the holy Ganges.

There was a festival going on when we arrived. People were celebrating the beginning of a four-day holiday celebrating the god Vishnu, the Great Preserver, who has woken from the four-month long hibernation that he requires each year. Garlands of flowers were strung across the Bagmati, and four naked little boys chased each other around the small white shrines that line the river's terraced left bank. Women on the temple side of the river were bathing with their sarees on, rinsing their mouths with water, rolling onto their sides in the murky slow current.

Just downstream from all the fun, a half-naked priest raked through the embers of a smoking cremation ghat. We watched from a distance as he poked at something black and egg-shaped. When we came closer to investigate, I saw that it was a human head—and the black, roasted remains of a torso, tiny and twisted. The head seemed to be thrown back in a gesture that was both agonized and inspired. There was something triumphant and ultimate about it, like a face contorted during childbirth.

"Where is that soul now?" Karen wondered. I knew the local answer. The spirit, blind and helpless, would have begun its passage through the Rivers of Fire, clinging to the tail of a sacred cow. Ah, the imagination that goes into creating what comes next! And the aching sigh of mortality: our smooth, warm bodies crackling into ash, skulls bursting with a pop, limbs falling away. We stood still and silent and watched the head in the flames, teeth grimacing at the sky.

"An inevitable turn of events, I'm afraid," I muttered.

And then I realized that, if you take away the words "I'm afraid," what I'd said was essentially Buddha's primary teaching: death is inevitable. The whole trick lies in somehow coming to terms with that fear.

What, I asked myself, is $650 if it can help me sizzle those two words—"I'm afraid"—out of my life? What price enlightenment? Is it a bargain basement commodity, or do you get it when and where you can, damn the expense?

I hailed a taxi and rushed back to the Oriental Art Emporium, full of conviction.

"Let me see the Buddha once more!" I cried. Babukaji handed it to me.

For a moment I was the happiest man in the world. But then it began: the inevitable Western-man slide into the various hells! What was that discoloration under the eye? Why was there an uneven section on the stomach? Hey, I didn't realize that it rocked a little bit! The base is uneven! Who ever heard of a Buddha that wasn't completely steady!?

SHADDUUP!

I stood there trembling, clasping my bulging wallet, poised on the brink of Actually Doing It.

"You know," Babukaji sagely declared, "this Buddha is a thing of very special beauty. It is worth many times what you are paying. I tell you this: if at any time in the future you wish to part with it, I will buy it back from you for the very amount you are spending today. So you need never fear that you have acted rashly."

Was I dreaming? A perfect $650 Buddha, with a money-back guarantee? I counted out the rupees—all 15,000 of them, in impressively large bills—and left the store with the prize under my arm.

18

Oh, my mind! Why do you hover so restlessly over the changing circumstances of life? Why do you make me so confused and restless? Why do you urge me to collect so many things? You are like a plow that breaks into pieces before beginning to plow; you are like a rudder that is dismantled just before venturing out on the sea!
Oh, my mind! Once you caused me to be born as a king, and then you caused me to be born as an outcast, and to beg for my food. Sometimes you cause me to be born in the heavenly mansions of the gods and to dwell in luxury and in ecstasy; then you plunge me into the flames of hell.
Oh, my foolish, foolish mind! Thus you have led me along different paths, and I have been obedient to you and docile. But now that I have heard the Buddha's teaching, do not disturb me any more or cause me further suffering. Let us seek enlightenment together—humbly and patiently.

—BUKKYO DENDO KYOKAI, *The Teaching of Buddha*

By 1987, Lalji had moved away from his chicken farm along the Bagmati River—the place where he had made his hasty pronouncement concerning the future of my mental health—and into an old Rana palace not far from Nag Pokhari. The Ranas, a greedy breed of fattened aristocrats with European pretensions, leeched Nepal for all it was worth from 1846 until 1950, at which point they were booted out of power by the current regime. Their most obvious contribution to the Kathmandu Valley was a smattering of hideously self-indulgent "palaces" that boiled up, replete with Greco-Roman columns and porticos, chandeliers, fountains, marble mosaic floors, and countless other manifestations of tasteless rococo madness, between the subtle brick houses and vegetable gardens of Kathmandu's inner-city neighborhoods.

Lalji's flat was the lower-left-hand corner of a relatively modest Rana atrocity. A plaster statue of a horse, right front leg, head, and tail broken off, stood by the entranceway steps. It was meant, I supposed, to face regally over the broad front lawn, now overgrown with weeds, and a large artificial pond that, carpeted in algae and percolating ominously, looked like a chemistry experiment gone horribly awry. The setting had the crumbled, postapocalyptic feeling of a *Planet of the Apes* film.

I found Lalji inside the house, casually attired in a blue Adidas sweatsuit. He was washing his face and rinsing out his mouth with long, meditative gurgles, not to be interrupted. But I was ready to supply my own entertainment. Using a rather bedraggled lawn chair that sat out in the front yard, I set to work with the props I'd brought along: a regulation daypack, a long-burning candle that I'd picked up from a sowji down the street, and my brand new Buddha.

While constructing my assemblage, I reflected on my previous visit, four years earlier. I had spent, if you added it all up, a fair amount of time performing the exercises he had recommended. My attempts weren't totally lame. Although I hadn't been able to envision actual flames, I thought I did perceive a kind of dull rippling effect, like what you might see across the surface of a road on a hot day. I was obsessed, though, with Lalji's promise of actual *light* and, producing none, could only jiggle these ripple effects with limited enthusiasm.

Yet I had, inevitably, returned to Lalji's once more—bent on proving that in 1987, eight years after his first brash comments about my work, I could at least answer his challenge to create a nonneurotic work of art. And so, while awaiting his appearance, I hastily fashioned a sort of conceptual sculpture, satisfied that even my limited progress with his dynamic form of finger-focused meditation had empowered me to create a work of art that was neither neurotic nor critical, but a bright and true reflection of the enlightened being that, with the help of Lalji and my new Buddha, I was bound to become.

Lalji finished his morning ablutions and greeted me, carrying two cane chairs. He spared only the briefest glance for the weird contraption that I had assembled. Before we even sat down I felt compelled to draw his full attention to it.

"This is the answer to your challenge," I said, certain that he would know exactly what I meant. "It's a sculpture I just made. It's called 'Mr. Jeffrey'."

I pointed to the lawn chair. My daypack, bulging with a mysterious load, was looped over its back. On the chair's right armrest, the candle I had brought—handily attached with a few drops of wax—burned almost invisibly in the morning light.

"Inside that daypack," I informed Lalji, well satisfied with my own imagination, "I have concealed something: a perfect statue of the Buddha that I bought down on New Road yesterday. The Buddha in the pack—so near to me, yet so hidden!—is within, concealed in the midst of the excess emotional baggage I carry around day after day. Ironic, eh?

Because as long as I keep groping blindly in front of me, I'll never find that hidden Buddha-nature!

"And the chair, of course, symbolizes relaxation. Perfect relaxation. Complete relaxation. While the flame, as you have instructed, serves as my personal cleansing element."

Lalji studied the assemblage, nodding thoughtfully, and we returned to our cane chairs. I carefully described my progress with the finger-flame exercises. He laughed with glee as I bemoaned my inability to produce actual, visible flames.

"But those waves, that rippling you perceive, is exactly what you are supposed to see!" His mustache curved upward, toward the rim of his woolen skullcap. "You can't expect to see real flames from sporadic practice! Those will come maybe after six months or one year of absolute diligence! What you are seeing is exactly right. Your progress thus far is superb."

I was doubtful, to say the least.

"You say that I can easily let go of my neuroses," I stammered, "yet I feel that they are weights that are somehow chained to me. Of course I would love to just be free of them—but they constitute memories of my childhood, of my parents, about 60 percent of my life and memory! It's not that easy!"

"It *is* easy," he said. "You just continue with the flames, and all your garbage will be consumed. What is the garbage, eh? It is broken plates, wasted rice, shit, scraps of flesh or wood? It makes no difference: just light a flame and they will all burn away. Your problems are like ledges of wax inside of you, blocking and diverting your energies. When you purge with your flames, they will simply melt away. And do not matter that the flames are small, just from your fingertips! Even a single match has the power to put all of Kathmandu in flames!

"And when your garbage is burned up, what need you carry?"

With these words Lalji rose from the straw chair and strolled, in no hurry, over to the construction I had assembled in his front yard. He regarded it with supreme disdain.

"Nothing!" He seized the daypack off the back rest, turned it upside down, and shook my new Buddha statue out onto the ground! I leaped from my seat.

"This pack that you have placed on this so-called sculpture"—he held it away from himself, as if it were a dead rat—"what does it contain? What does it hold? Nothing but the garbage of your past and the garbage of your future!"

With an accurate swing of his arm, he hurled the tattered rucksack into the fetid little pond, which swallowed it up with an obscene sucking noise. I could only gape in amazement. And then he picked up—*the Buddha!*—my proud, priceless Buddha with the money-back guarantee!!

"Even this Buddha—this too is garbage! It is not Buddha!" He weighed it in his hand, like a chicken. "It is just molded metal, dirt, paint, nothing but trash! Stop carrying this garbage around with you everywhere!" I croaked, certain he was about to do the *unthinkable*—and I would have dived in right after it—but instead he heaved the Buddha, underhand, in my direction. I caught it and held it protectively to my chest.

"If I were to grab your pack out of that shitty lake," he said contemptuously, "*then* I would have in my hands a true sculpture: completely garbage! But at this point you can only sculpt illusion and conflict; not even full garbage!

"But supposing you continue with these exercises. What if, after a while, you are cleansed? What need then of the candle or the flame? You may dispense with these as well!"

Lalji reached down, snapped the candle from its moorings and threw it—*thrulp*—into the pond. "What need for cleansing if you are already clean?"

"Guh, guh, guh, guh, guh. . . ."

"And once you have reached this point, look!" He stretched his arms toward the lawn chair, an expression of mock astonishment on his face. "You have only an empty chair! But now you won't even need a chair to relax! You will be relaxed anywhere, in any position! You won't need to be sitting down on something!"

He picked up the chair, got a grip on it, and, spinning around like a shot-putter, hurled it off to the side of the yard.

"So then what?" he cried. "You can come to me and say, 'See, Lalji, there is my sculpture! There it is!'" He gestured at the empty space where the chair had been. "'It's right there!'

"And if I can perceive it, fine! And if not—well, at least you have created something truly reflective of your cleansed mind and your cleansed body. At that point I withdraw my challenge. At that point you will be, one hundred percent, a complete man—and a complete artist."

19

Shortly before taking my leave of Nepal, seeking an evening's diversion, I called up my friend Elliot—he manages the SEVA Nepal Blindness Program—and asked if he felt like stepping out on the town with me. He was more than agreeable. We conspired to drive down to the Soaltee Oberoi and squander a few rupees in the evil Casino Nepal before steeping ourselves in the hotel's luxurious sauna. Then we'd head out to a Chinese restaurant and round off the evening at Flo's Place—a private club catering to members of the U.S. community abroad—for some homestyle entertainment.

At Elliot's request, I telephoned Flo's and asked the Nepali receptionist which video would be showing.

"Donée," he replied.

"Hmmm. Is this some French film?"

"No, no, no, American."

"Oh, yeah? Gee, it must've come out since I've been away. Can you spell it?"

"Yasss. *D-U-N-E.*"

Elliot picked me up in his indefatigable Volkswagen bug. We spent a moment contemplating the crow—by now utterly wretched, indescribable, an apparition out of H. P. Lovecraft—and set off for an evening of high jinks on the highways and byways of Kathmandu: the Clumsy Cosmopolis. The Sudden Metropolis. We gambled away nickles and dimes in the slimy Casino, sweated meditatively over salted lemon sodas in the Soaltee Oberoi's steam room, and dined on hot and sour soup at the Hotel de l'Annapurna's Chinese restaurant. We wound up our night on the town at Flo's and sat through as much of *Dune* as we could stand, treating ourselves to imported Budweisers from the commissary-stocked bar. Elliot drove me home around 1 A.M. and stopped in for a slice of pumpkin pie before chugging off into the night.

It was not until late the following day, running around town on some semi-official errand, that I made the horrible discovery: sometime during the previous night, somewhere between the Casino, steam room, restaurant, and Flo's, I had done the unthinkable. I had lost my brown nylon neck pouch, and with it my passport, airline ticket, and vaccination record.

The search that ensued was desperate, complete, and fruitless. I grilled the staff at the Soaltee, lifted cushions at Flo's, tore apart Elliot's Volkswagen and reduced my room at home to a disaster area of jumbled clothing, books, and camping gear. Nothing. This was impossible. It couldn't be happening to me. Scheduled to leave in less than a week, and all my documentation gone!

It was classic. I eventually passed through all the stages—denial, anger, grieving, resignation—all the steps attendant to lethal loss that Elisabeth Kübler-Ross describes in what might be called the "American Book of the Dead." Finally, having abandoned all hope, I found myself engulfed by a misty feeling of . . . *nothingness*. Of blurring at the edges. My very identity seemed to be at stake. It was as if I'd been hurled into the Bardo, the nether world, a naked man without a planet.

It was this general sense of discombobulation, I later theorized, that set me up for what was to happen next.

On the northwestern rim of the Kathmandu Valley, there is a high, knuckle-shaped peak called Jamachok. It's a long hike to get there—up through the Nagarjun Forest, picking your way through brush and trees—but worth it. From the bald crest of the peak, a rusting metal tower provides a giddy panorama of the entire valley, and the Himalayas beyond— from the dark pyramid of Everest in the east to the rugged Ganesh Range in the west.

On the patchy, littered grass just below the tower, a few whitewashed shrines pay homage to ancient Bipaswi—the first of all the human Buddhas.

Eons ago, when the Kathmandu Valley was a placid lake inhabited by Snake Gods, Bipaswi settled down in deep meditation on Jamachok Peak. One night, as the full moon of April rose over the eastern foothills, he took from the folds of his robe a tiny seed and tossed it into the water.

Moonlight bent into ripples. By morning, a thousand-petaled lotus had blossomed on the lake's surface, cradling a miraculous flame that attracted pilgrims from all over Central Asia. These devotees included the bodhisattva Manjushri, who finally drained the great lake and prepared the valley for human habitation.

I spent an entire morning hiking up through the Nagarjun Forest to Jamachok, sweating buckets in the inexplicable November heat. My water bottle, pathetically inadequate, was drained long before I reached the summit. In order to survive, it would be necessary to cultivate a lizard mentality: dry, still, and watchful, in need of nothing but the most occasional sustenance.

Now that the primary distraction in my life—shopping for a perfect Buddha—had been tamed, I felt I had very little to concern myself with. There were, I must admit, the usual questions on my mind: questions about my career in general, and about my eternally postponed novel in particular. But these could wait.

What I craved was an afternoon of easy contemplation in the vivid valley sunlight, high above the push-come-to-shove of urban Asia. It might loosen things up in me. Who could tell? After all, this peak was a mythically famous *chakra*-sharpener: extraordinarily fertile ground for action, growth, explosion. Long ago, Bipaswi had sown a fateful seed from atop Jamachok Peak; perhaps the pollen of inspiration was still in the air.

To make myself more receptive to these subtle influences, I had brought along a single pipeful of potent Nepali hashish, grown in the shadow of the towering Annapurnas, along the banks of the wild Kali Gandaki River. It was holy herb, impregnated with the same deep molecular structures of Himalayan air, water, fire, and soil. I had obtained it from the son of a village lama in exchange for a Star Trek T-shirt.

Arriving at Jamachok Peak, I immediately climbed to the top of the lookout tower. Lines of colorful Tibetan prayer flags, webbed between the tower's legs and the trees below, fluttered in the breeze.

The air was unusually clear, and, standing on the edge of that spindly tower half a mile above the city, I experienced a sudden surge of vertigo. I felt as if I were suspended in a hang-glider, soaring over the foothills and swooping down into the vast, bowl-shaped valley. Far below, I could make out the tiny spindle of Bhimsen Tower, and the sugar cube of the Royal Palace. Swayambhunath gleamed from its hillock like a gold-capped tooth. Searching further east, I found the white dome of Bodhnath stupa and watched the leisurely

143

ballet of takeoff and landing at Tribhuvan International Airport.

And then my gaze was pulled outward, upward, toward the ragged white profile of the infinite Himalayas. The sight of those mountains struck a chord that resonated in the back of my head and the center of my chest. I longed for them, awed and aching, utterly seduced by their cold and perfect mountainness.

This was it. This was all there was. My entire life had conspired to bring me to this particular point. Sitting down on on the tower's graffiti-covered deck, I pulled out my wooden pipe and sprinkled a few chunks of ganja into the bowl.

I watched the clouds. They were unlike anything I'd ever seen, unlike any clouds that had ever appeared over the Western world. Tiny meringued peaks, curled at the tip, golden against the electric blue sky. Like the stylized flames in a Tibetan thangka painting. They were the kinds of flames that I had often seen surrounding the dreadful Bhairab—the wrathful, bloodthirsty guardian deity with huge eyes and gleaming fangs, who dances in a halo of scarlet, gold-tipped flames.

My eyes shifted to the prayer flags. Most were all but transparent, worn down to bare gauze. Only the gossamer essences of their forms and colors remained. As I watched them shiver in the breeze, watched them point and snap, I thought I could see the prayers themselves rising up, radiating outward with that same shimmering ripple effect that had flowed from my fingers during Lalji's exercise.

It seemed to me that there was some mystical secret in there somewhere—some profound link between power and prayer that I might be able to grab the tail of. But it jumped around like a kite, and I couldn't get a grip on it. Maybe in writing, I thought. Maybe if I try to write about it, everything will sort itself out.

I reached into my pack, found my journal, and opened up to a blank page. But when I tried to write, all that emerged from my pen were big, bubble-shaped letters, as huge as deformed cells. After a single, cartoony sentence I abandoned the effort.

I leaned back against the tower, shivered, and closed my eyes. When I opened them again, the line I had written was pulsing within a neon nimbus of color. It was beautiful, but somehow terrifying, and before I got halfway into my second sentence my hand just slid spastically off the paper. And then I was off—crashing through the cerebral ceiling into the highest, scariest place I'd ever been.

Flaming, multicolored dragons battled in the clouds above my head, and the gentle galloping of the prayer flags had become a stampede.

Where was I? What was going on here? I was panting, and my heart was hammering in my chest. My tongue flopped around my mouth like an unpeeled banana. Panic symptoms. There was no point fighting; I had to roll with it, find a channel for the wild energy that was pumping pure adrenaline through my veins. Suddenly I knew what I needed to bring me down—exercise! I jumped to my feet and stretched my arms upward, breathing deeply as my whole body shuddered.

Stretch, stretch, stretch . . . oooff . . . to the limit. Ooooh, it felt good. I could hear my joints cracking, the muscles shuffling into place. But then I spread my legs apart, as far as they would go, and I immediately had this horrible, vivid image of Bhairab grabbing me by the legs, and splitting me in half like a wishbone!

Aieeeeee! An electrifying current went ripping up through my body, groin to skull, and zoomed toward outer space. Before I knew what was happening, my entire body began to shake violently, vibrating uncontrollably.

And then the wind picked up. That's the only way I can describe it. But this wasn't the same wind that was flickering through the prayer flags, or sculpting the clouds; not even close. This was a violent and inexorable wind, supernatural, as if gravity itself was being reversed. It was a solar hurricane, and as it got stronger and stronger I realized that I was about five seconds from being blown right off the lookout tower and into empty space, a mile above the sprawling Kathmandu Valley!

I grabbed the window frame of the lookout tower and hung on for dear life, legs flailing out behind me. This was what it must feel like to be sucked out of a commercial airliner—clinging desperately to the arm of a tourist-class seat as your body flaps toward eternity like a giant wind sock.

And as I hung suspended, arms wrapped desperately around the tower, I was struck by an almost comical sense of déjà-vu. Gosainkund! This was just like that awful storm at Gosainkund! Because I knew, I *knew*, that if I dared to let go I would simply blow away—and explode like a trillion tiny pieces of confetti, raining down all over the mountains and valleys, never to be put back together again.

Then, just as suddenly as it had started, the mysterious wind died down. All was still. I found myself on my knees, gasping for breath, T-shirt clinging to my back. Slowly, gingerly, I released my hold on the tower—and in a desperate bid to reach terra firma I stood up and staggered, on rubber legs, down the metal steps.

I flopped myself on the ledge of Bipaswi's small white shrine, utterly spent. From atop the little stupa, the painted

146

eyes of Buddha gazed benevolently out over the hillside. It certainly seemed a safer home port than the tower. . . . Trying to calm myself, I took one breath . . . another breath . . . everything was going to be all right. I closed my eyes—pressed my fingers against the bridge of my nose—when Boom! Off went my brain, right over the crest of another hair-raising roller coaster ride!

WWWHHHHOA!

Something enormous grabbed me by the scruff of my neck, and before I had any idea what was going on I felt myself being dragged off—pulled up an endless, magnificent stairway—to meet God.

God. The name sounded familiar. . . . Then I remembered: four years ago, trekking alone through the Arun Valley in far eastern Nepal. It was one those perfect spring days, the grass Oz-green, the sky like Earth's own blue eye, strange birds darting over the terraced hillsides like fighting kites. I was hiking back to Tumlingtar, high as a kite myself, carrying a full pack and listening to Kitaro's *Silk Road* on my Sony Walkman. The music had that hypnotic, canting rhythm of religion to it. I found myself singing. Not songs; psalms. I hiked along the empty trail inventing psalms, addressing them to the Lord, as tears of absolute infant happiness rolled into my beard.

About 45 minutes later—just as the tape ran out—I came around a sharp corner and stopped in my tracks. A perfect bouquet of wildflowers lay in the center of the trail, tied neatly with a piece of red string. I knew exactly whom they were from.

God! The big *G!* I was hauled relentlessly upward in a dizzying spiral, my feet dragging behind me. Huge mandalas and dancing thunderbolts loomed on the edges of my vision, racing through kaleidoscopic riffs. Fireworks exploded around me with bicentennial frenzy, seeming to come from every direction. I kept trying to blink, forgetting that my eyes were already closed.

And how did I feel as I was being pulled like a sacrificial goat into the Holy Presence? Ashamed! Underdressed! Who would ever think of meeting God in tattered shorts, sneakers, and a sweaty T-shirt? It was like one of those dreams where you have to give a big speech to a roomful of VIPs and realize too late that you've left the house in your underwear.

Up and up we went—until at last, somewhere up there, high on some breathless level of the collective consciousness, we stopped. A golden doorway in front of me burst open. I cried out, reeling back from the blinding, shimmering light—but was thrown into the chamber like a rag doll, stumbling to my knees.

There was a gigantic burst of wind and flame, and a mighty voice coming from inside and outside of everything roared,

"So, Mr. Jeffrey—what do you have to say for yourself?"

Say? What to say? I went spinning through my brain for the right words, the right prayers, the right questions, because I knew that this was it: my long-fantasized chance to have a tête-à-tête with God, to collect the Ultimate Blessing right from the Source! It was the opportunity of a lifetime, and I didn't want to blow it—but my mouth was dry, so dry, that all I could do was croak, in a small, pathetic voice: "Thank you!"

It sounded right, so I said it again—and again—realizing, as I continued to utter those two words, that I had lit on a great secret, had collected a fabulous blessing, entirely by chance. I had discovered my personal holy mantra; the incantation that would save me whenever I felt tempted by the luxury of self-pity, or distracted by the affectation of self-doubt. Not only was it my mantra; it was the ultimate, the highest mantra of all!

Not only was it the highest mantra; it was the *only* mantra.

"Well, you're welcome!" God roared.

That was it! Time to go! Without a moment to spare for an autograph or a handshake, I was torn from The Presence—and opened my eyes, astounded to find that I was still leaning against old Bipaswi's shrine, facing directly into the sun.

At that very point—for reasons that might be obvious to the greenest psychologist, but which continue to elude me— I decided to do a very insidious thing to myself. From that high ground of insight and spirituality, fresh from my apocalyptic encounters with Lalji and God, I decided to ask myself

The
Big
Question.

Nothing less than a direct confrontation about what ultimately emerged, at that moment, as the single, central, and most crucial decision of my life. I mean, as long as I was in the neighborhood. . . .

"Okay, Mister. So what about it?" I asked myself. "Are you going to write this great big novel of yours or not? Hunh? Hunh? Hunh? Because if you are, man, just say yes and *do* it—right now—starting *this minute!*"

In one fell swoop, all the demons of impatience that had been percolating in me for years came bubbling to the surface. I saw myself as an old man: pathetic and hobbling, with nothing of any enduring value accomplished. No marriage, no children, that damned novel I'd been promising myself I'd write still unwritten, death racing nearer by the instant.

"Hunh? Hunh? Yes or no?"

All I had to do was mutter one syllable. Yes or no. Yes, and no more stalling; or no, and no more self-torture about the When and the If. This was it—do or die—now or never. Face to face with myself and no turning away.

But I sat there, paralyzed. I could not make a sound. And from that nadir of shame, right in the middle of this potential betrayal of all my illusions of literary greatness and self-importance, something caught my eye.

I looked up—

—and saw a tiny scrap of something that looked like confetti, drifting down from somewhere on high. Drifting down like a little wing, and coming to rest among the candy wrappers and empty cigarette boxes and scraps of toilet paper on the sloping grass, about ten feet from where I was sitting.

I stood and walked over to it. And then I realized: it wasn't a scrap of litter. Not at all. It was a tiny prayer, in Tibetan, printed on a little salmon-colored piece of paper. Just a tiny prayer flag, hardly recognizable in the midst of all that trash.

I peered at it, stunned.

"That scrap of paper," a voice whispered, "is all that you are: one small, pink note against the endless expanse of clutter. So make a big question out of your book, or make a little question out of it. But never forget one thing. When it all comes down to dust, nothing that you or anyone else on Earth can create is anything more or less than a gasp in the wind: one prayer scattered among billions of others, all equally holy, and all eaten at last by the rain and the wind."

20

People call one phase of the moon a full moon, they call
another phase a crescent moon; in reality, the moon is always perfectly round, neither waxing nor waning.
Buddha is precisely like the moon. In the eyes of men
and women Buddha may seem to change in appearance
but, in truth, Buddha does not change.
— BUKKYO DENDO KYOKAI, *The Teaching of Buddha*

Tribhuvan International Airport. A week before the shortest
day of the year. Late afternoon and it was already dark and
cold, and as I checked in at the pissy-smelling old terminal
it was impossible to believe that a sleek, hi-tech jetliner
would shortly taxi up the runway and whisk me off to some
highly efficient, consummately industrialized society.

It hadn't been easy to get my ticket re-issued—I learned
what would be my final lesson about flying Korean Airlines—but it finally did come through, after a few phone calls
made, at my request, by the unusually sympathetic U.S. Embassy.

I paid my departure tax, displayed my passport—brand
new, issued only days before—and brought my carry-on luggage over to the customs table. I yawned; there are few
things more satisfying than knowing you are clean, totally
and indisputably legal.

"What do you have in that sack?"

"Oh, daju, not much. Some film; a couple of cameras; and a statue of the Buddha."

"May we please see it? The Buddha?"

"With pleasure." I fetched it out and gave it over to the officer to admire. Who could fail to be impressed by this work of art? By its complacent expression, its demure smile, its remarkable workmanship?

He turned it over in his hands a few times, then gave me a look of deep sympathy.

"I'm sorry, sir! This statue has no clearance tags!"

"Eh? What?"

I turned white. He was right! Amid all the confusion over my lost passport and ticket, I had neglected to stop in at the Department of Archaeology to pick up the necessary stamp!

The irony of my situation was so extreme—so Asian—that I instinctively looked on either side of me, trying to find some other Westerner to share it with. Since ancient art, as well I knew, was being smuggled out of Nepal left and right, the government has mandated that all antique objects must be cleared by the Department of Archaeology before they can leave the kingdom. The process is simple: you simply haul your purchase to the D of A office, pay a minuscule fee, and receive a wax-sealed stamp certifying that the object is less than a hundred years old.

One of the first things my art-smuggling research revealed, of course, was that the procedure is a big joke; anybody with money or influence can get a clearance stamp faster than you can say "torana."

"Aw, come on," I sputtered, feeling myself about to slide into some Fellini-esque drama. "Come on, now, you can see that this Buddha isn't old! It's brand new! Look, it's by Sidhi Raj!"

152

"How do I know that? Where is the signature?"

I turned the statue over, hoping beyond hope that Nancy's Buddha had not been a fluke; maybe the Patan craftsman had begun to make a practice of signing his works. But no—there was nothing on the base but the impression of a little lotus.

"I'm sorry, sir. I am only doing my duty!" The customs agent gauged my distress and adopted a more conciliatory tone. "Please; we will not destroy this Buddha. We will only hold it. The next time you return to Nepal, no problem. You just get the proper tags, and we will let you through without a second glance!"

I raged; I moaned; I begged and pleaded. Finally it was just him and me, staring at each other: a total stalemate.

Well, I thought. Well. It seemed futile and inappropriate to lash out with my fists, although that was definitely the primal inspiration. So I tried a few deep breaths, and a silent prayer, instead.

God grant me the serenity to know what I can't change . . . and I determined, with a little snort of insight, that this had to be some kind of a test. I mean, think about it. Wasn't yet another crucial teaching of the Buddha—non-attachment—being offered up to me in one not-so-easy lesson?

A tinny loudspeaker clapped into the gloom: "Final call for Flight 650 to Bangkok, please board immediately at Gate Number 2! Royal Nepal Airlines Flight 650 to Bangkok, boarding immediately at Gate Number 2. . . ."

"Kay garnay," I muttered: what to do. "Take it, daju. Hold it. Keep it. Enjoy it," I said. "After all, that isn't really the Buddha—no, daju—it's just molded metal, dirt, paint, . . . nothing but trash!"

And then I laughed, a dizzy, what-the-hell laugh, and my whole body contracted with an enormous sense of release—as if I'd come to the end of a very long book, long and confusing, but suddenly all the jigsaw pieces were spliced together by a few completely unexpected words.

I had lost the Buddha; but I had won the war.

This was it. I took a deep breath. "Namasté," I said to the customs agent. "And *Ramro sanga basnos*—" Remain here with all my blessings.

"Namasté," he replied. Then he smiled, and, after a quick glance from side to side, handed me back the Buddha.

I stared at him, knees weakening, and croaked out one word: "Why?"

"Maybe, I think, you have an honest face."

21

It was a night flight from Kathmandu to Hong Kong. A clear, brilliant December night, and by the time the flight took off—we were delayed, as usual—the moon had risen above the black spires of the Himalayas and was gleaming off the snow.

We circled the valley, and the lights of the runway got smaller. From outer space, Kathmandu looks like anywhere else—sodium yellow along the avenues, spotlit factories, the headlights of Japanese cars crawling across the earth. The dull, phosphorescent glow of civilization.

It was all down there: my entire other life. Those wise and funny people and great gods and goddesses; those shuttered shopwindows full of fantastic, expensive Buddhas. And so much more! I looked down and tried to imagine the black cows sleeping in darkened streets, the rickshaw drivers huddled in their carts beneath the temples of Asan Tole, the musicians chanting ballads in the bandstand at Chhetrapati. And I imagined a black crow, festering and precarious, awaiting its inevitable rendezvous with gravity. . . .

The previous evening, an hour before midnight, I had left the house for a final stroll through Kathmandu. I walked past silent Nag Pokhari—Snake Lake—and caught a creaking rickshaw down to Asan Tole, the central market district.

Ahh, the night: so fine for wandering, so deep and amber and sharply etched, lit from a hundred unlikely directions at once. Time and again I could have sworn it was stage lighting, and that I had wandered onto a Hollywood set, or into a dream. Every alley was a nook-filled diorama, ancient and crumbling yet awkwardly modern, still off balance after the past decade's rough shove toward Westernization.

It was a full moon—always a puja night somewhere in Kathmandu. Even at that late hour I encountered half a dozen troupes of musicians, chanting in the bandstands; parades of singing worshipers bearing statues of Laksmi and Ganesh into otherwise empty Asan Tole, their arrival preceded by pairs of pirouetting ragtag kids spinning around in crazy ballroom-style dance; cymbals beating, horns bleating, the incandescent bulbs hanging along the narrow avenue swinging in the breeze and casting spastic shadows, everything looking as if it had sprung directly out of the soil of Nepal itself. I was caught short, wondering how I manage to live without that riptide of spirituality back in the United States.

After the final parade had passed I sat down on a step at the crooked elbow of a dark and totally unfamiliar little avenue, leaning against a shuttered doorway. The street was so bafflingly twisted and funky that it might have inspired a drawing by M. C. Escher or Dr. Seuss. But then a strange and singular little Ganesh shrine caught my eye—bent metal banners leaning from a battered brass roof—and I realized to my astonishment that this surreal, empty corner was, by day, the same manic marketplace where I had shopped for incense, herbal toothpaste, kitchen pans, and cotton blankets during the past few months. And as I sat there, marveling at the seemingly impossible transformation, the whole catalog of disguises that Kathmandu slips into and out of suddenly flashed across my inner eye with dizzying, flipbook animation.

A city, I realized, becomes far more than a passive repository of its people; it can also play the role of magus, mask dancer, and sage.

The stewardess walked by, offering hard little candies. I took a red one and popped it into my mouth, as if it were a pill that would help me weather culture shock. Tomorrow morning I would wake up in Hong Kong, have a cup of coffee, and give myself plenty of time to think about how terrible and exciting it was to return to the United States of America. Back to California, where the wonderfully skewed psychology of Asia would slip slowly out of my mind. Back to the cold, cold rain, bumper-to-bumper traffic on the bridges, Thai food, and television; back to the land of tightly wrapped people, barren avenues, extortionate prices, answering machines.

Right now, just the idea of it exhausted me. I leaned against my window and peered into the night.

Then I jumped—somewhere due north of the Kathmandu Valley, high above the foothills, a brilliant flash caught my eye—and I saw, for two brief seconds, the huge silver cornea of the gibbous moon.

It blinked at me, brilliant as a diamond, reflected in the icy waters of Gosainkund Lake.

A Brief Political Postscript

Several weeks after my departure from Kathmandu, the king also left Nepal. He was off for a short visit to the Maldives, where the royal family owns a small island with a fully appointed estate, just in case.

The most direct route, or at least the best paved road, between the Royal Palace and the airport passes right by the compound that I had lived in with Ray Rodney and Krishna.

A few hours before the king's passage, crews of low-caste sweeper women were stationed along every meter of the road. Squatting low, they swung their short brooms in wide arcs over the pavement. The yellow dumpsters of the Solid Waste Management Program were trucked away; piles of crumbling bricks were shoveled out of sight; dog-doo was removed. Around Ray's house, weeds were pulled up and a fresh coat of whitewash was heaved onto the soot-blackened compound wall. When the hour approached, a neatly uniformed policeman carrying a polished *lathi* club rang the doorbell and warned Krishna and Raj not to venture outside for the next half hour or so.

In all their zeal to tidy up the roadway, the legions of cleanliness had never bothered to look up, directly above their heads. It was to prove a fateful oversight.

At precisely 10:45 A.M. the king's Mercedes limousine, packed with handsomely monogrammed luggage and accompanied by a full escort, left the Royal Palace. The convoy sped down Lazimpat, past the ranks of saluting police officers and curious onlookers. It sailed past the cinema, whose banks of snack sellers had been concealed behind a tall hedge, and moved up the hill to loop around Nag Pokhari, Snake Lake, the mercurial surface of which had been skimmed of the slimy green algae that, left to its own devices, would have soon crawled from the pond to terrorize downtown Kathmandu.

The motorcade approached the compound. The Television Nepal van passed our front gate; then came a bank of motorcycle escorts, a car with a red light revolving on its roof, and another couple of motorcycles, followed at last by the sleek white limousine.

At the precise instant that the king's Mercedes drove past the compound, a fruit that had been ripening on the vine for a number of weeks decided to take the plunge. The unspeakable dead crow fell from its wire, rotted through at the "hip" joints, and burst against the windshield of the royal limousine in an explosion of dried blood, moldy feathers, and maggots. The astonished driver immediately threw the washer-wiper switch. Needless to say, the blades acted more like spatulas than squeegees, spreading the jellied mass evenly across the glass.

"Stop the car," the king demanded.

Sri Sri Sri Sri Sri Maharaja Birendra Bir Bikram Shah Dev opened the door and stepped from the Mercedes. He looked up and saw the bleached, bony crow's legs dangling from the wire. He looked at them for a long time; and then his gaze wandered. He saw the clumsily patched brick wall of a nearby schoolyard. He saw barefoot girls in ragged dresses standing in doorways, baby brothers and sisters perched on their narrow hips. He saw the greasy rear ends of three-wheeled tempo cabs and broken-down rickshaws that had been crammed, ostensibly out of sight, behind a nearby building.

The king gazed all around, at the scores of incredulous faces staring at him from crooked windows and precarious rooftops. A dog broke free from its rope and ran across the street to piss against a nearby wall. A little boy waved from a doorway. The king stared at the boy—who was immediately grabbed by his terrified mother—and waved back. A breeze of amazed giggles filled the air from all directions, and within five seconds every boy and girl within eyeshot was waving wildly to His Majesty, flailing like an anemone in hopes of a royal response. . . .

The king began to walk. He walked away from his motorcade and toward Nag Pokhari, followed by half a dozen disbelieving police and army officers. He wandered past the abandoned cement ping-pong tables, a padlocked bicycle shop, and a grove of thriving marijuana bushes. This was the edge of the neat little set that had been prepared for him. But the king did not stop there; he crossed through a scraggly little park that led onto Naxal Avenue. Though only two blocks from the palace grounds, he might just as well have been on the moon. Like a sleepwalker who has suddenly awakened into a totally unexpected environment, the king continued up the hushed street, roving unchained into the startled morning miasma of urban Kathmandu.

Okay, okay; it didn't happen that way. There was no such fantastic confluence of gravity and official traffic. No puréed crow served on polished Mercedes windshield. No giggling children peering down at His Majesty from the wooden window frames of Naxal and Nag Pokhari. No impromptu stroll. . . .

But happen it did; and with a degree of speed and violence that I could never have imagined as I was completing this book.

Shopping for Buddhas was not written as a political study. But it's not fiction either. The sections of the book that deal with politics are an accurate study of what the political climate was like in that country when I wrote them—and would probably have remained accurate, I believed, for at least the next few years.

But we live in extraordinary times, and things change extraordinarily fast. As this book goes to print—in April of 1990—Kathmandu is witnessing a series of astonishing events that may forever change the political structure of that Himalayan kingdom, and thus render (thankfully) my stern comments about Nepal's human rights violations and long political stagnation obsolete.

First, a bit of background. I visited Nepal once again in the early summer of 1989. The central motive for the trip was the final rewrite of *Shopping for Buddhas*. I was also there, however, to write about the "trade and transit" deadlock between Nepal and India. Rajiv Gandhi, irked by Nepal's increasingly friendly overtures toward China, had closed down thirteen of fifteen border crossings linking India with the kingdom, and set up harassing checkpoints at the remaining two.

Nepal, a landlocked country, relies absolutely on its overland routes through India. Shipments of everything from petrol and kerosene to aspirin and Chinese silk are trucked to Kathmandu from the ports at Calcutta. The Indian action, effectively an embargo, brought life in the kingdom to a virtual standstill for months.

His Majesty the King, perhaps afraid of being forced into a compromise (Hindu kings do not compromise), remained conspicuously mum on the issue. He dug himself ever deeper into his foxhole of formality, emerging only to issue banal edicts calling for solidarity in the face of hardship.

Nepal, home to some of the most enterprising, ingenious, and headstrong peoples in Asia, was adrift. Marooned. Lost at sea. And the handful of cosmetic improvements that the government had completed in the interests of "modernization"—the paved roads, traffic lights, television station, and elegant new International Terminal—were fooling nobody.

When I arrived in Nepal a final time in late 1989, India's new prime minister, V. P. Singh, was showing a more conciliatory tone toward Nepal. By early 1990 the year-long embargo was ending, and relations between the vast democracy and its quirky sibling were on their way back to "normal."

But something strange was in the air. There was a breeze, and a strong breeze, of deep and general disillusion and discontent. Some Nepalis bitterly ridiculed King Birendra's much-touted "Zone of Peace" foreign policy, defining Nepal instead as a "Zone of Passivity." They noted, with ill-concealed alarm, that with His Majesty perpetually silent and the cabinet festering with corruption, there was literally no one minding the store.

And things got worse. Rumors began to spread that the King, in need of some ready cash, had sold Nagarjun Forest. Sold it! To whom? Why, to the Nepali people, of course! His Majesty's asking price (non-negotiable, we may assume) was reportedly close to $30 million—a sum that was duly extracted from the national treasury, placed in the Royal Family's European bank accounts, and used to pay off a Greek island and military (that is, evacuation-style) helicopter.

Whether this was true or not doesn't matter. The astonishing thing is that people were willing to believe it. And they were becoming very, very annoyed.

"I can't think of any place," one educated art historian had told me in the spring of 1989, "where a bloodless, peaceful revolution would be easier to achieve. Nepal is so totally dependent on international aid, and on foreign exchange from tourism! If we could only get 10,000 people to parade down the streets, demanding constitutional rights and a multiparty system, the government would be so terrified of bad publicity that they would give in to our demands at once!"

This hopeful theory proved horribly wrong when, in late February of 1990, pro-democracy demonstrations were launched throughout the kingdom. The protesters—mostly students—were met with brutal police resistance. Before the month was out, an estimated thirty-three people had been killed. Thousands of peaceful demonstrators and suspected "agitators" were arrested, and thrown into dank, subterranean holding cells.

The Nepalese, a calm and non-confrontational people, were horrified. When I left Nepal at the beginning of March, the atmosphere was rife with tension. Bands of riot police roamed the streets. Wildcat strikes were paralyzing the cities; foreign embassies were issuing stern warnings to the government; and the ever-taciturn king, long given the benefit of the doubt, was falling dangerously out of favor with his subjects.

In late March, the cork exploded from the bottle. Demanding multiparty democracy, a new constitution, and guaranteed human rights, tens of thousands of Nepalis spilled out onto the streets of Kathmandu, Bhaktapur, and Patan—barricading roads, digging trenches and conducting mass demonstrations. But now the protesters were not limited to students and other "divisive elements." Doctors and nurses marched in silence outside their hospitals; teachers left their classrooms; and pilots of Royal Nepal Airlines, the monarchy-owned flagship carrier, stunned the Royal Palace by staging a one-day wildcat strike.

Once more, the demonstrators were met with sometimes deadly force. This time, however, they did not retreat. Pressure on the king increased; and on the morning of Friday, April 6th, Sri Panch Maharaja Birendra Bir Bikram Shah Dev appeared on Nepal television to announce a program of reforms for the Himalayan kingdom. These would include freeing of most political prisoners, drafting a new constitution, and dissolution of his present, corrupt cabinet.

Nowhere in his statement, though, did the king touch upon his people's pivotal demand: a multiparty democracy that would place Nepal in step with the modern world.

That same afternoon, an enormous crowd—hundreds of thousands of Nepalis—assembled near the Tundhikhel Parade Ground and began moving toward Durbar Marg. When they were some five hundred yards from the palace, troops guarding the royal nest fired tear gas; but the winds carried the noxious fumes back toward the police. The crowd continued to move forward—and the troops lowered their rifles and fired. At least fifty people were killed immediately, although witnesses reported hundreds of deaths, and hundreds more wounded.

The point of no return had been reached. For the next two days, a twenty-four-hour curfew was placed on most towns in Nepal. Police were ordered to shoot violators on sight. On Sunday, the people of Kathmandu defied the curfew, spilling once again onto the streets.

The crown had finally fallen—this time for real. And King Birendra seemed to realize the fact. On the evening of Sunday, April 8th, he appeared once again on Nepal television: this time to announce the lifting of the thirty-year ban on political parties, and Nepal's entry into the world of democratic nations. And once again Nepalis poured out onto the avenues: banging pans, setting off fireworks, singing and dancing.

Democracy will be a long and difficult road for the Nepalese. A country suffering from so much poverty and illiteracy cannot reform overnight. What the future (or even the next few months!) will bring, no one can predict. But one thing, at least, seems certain: the festering mess that has hovered over Nepal's head for so long has burst. The awful waiting has ended; and the process of cleaning up must begin.

Jeff Greenwald
April 9, 1990
Oakland, California